Celebrations

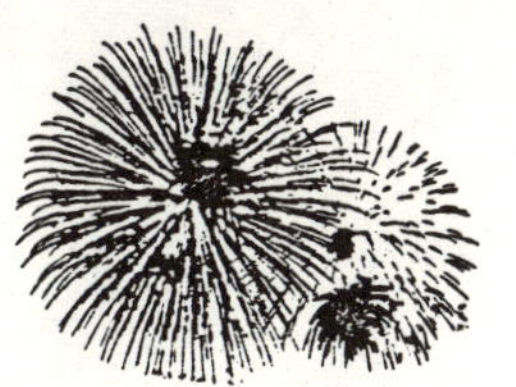

Celebrations

AMERICA'S BEST FESTIVALS, JAMBOREES, CARNIVALS & PARADES

JUDITH YOUNG
Foreword by Ray Bradbury

CAPRA PRESS
Santa Barbara

Cover photo by Cara Moore.
Cover and book design by Francine Rudesill.
Typography by Jim Cook Typography.

Special acknowledgement to Richard Gallen.

LIBRARY OF CONGRESS CATALOGING-IN-PUBLICATION-DATA
Young, Judith, 1940-
CELEBRATIONS:
America's best festivals, jamborees, carnivals, and parades.
(American holidays; v.1)
1. Festivals—United States—Directories.
2. Festivals—Canada—Directories.
I. Title.   II.   Series
GT4803.Y68   1985   394'.5'0973   85-22413
ISBN 0-88496-242-3 (pbk.)

Published by
CAPRA PRESS
Post Office Box 2068
Santa Barbara, Ca. 93120

CONTENTS

Foreword by Ray Bradbury 9

New England Celebrations

WINTER

Snodeo (Rangeley, ME) 19
White, White World (Kingfield, ME) 19
Dartmouth Winter Carnival (Hanover, NH) 20

SPRING

Fishermen's Festival (Boothbay Harbor, ME) 20
Vermont Maple Festival (St. Albans, VT) 21
Gaspee Days (Warwick, RI) 21
Wool Days (Old Sturbridge Village, MA) 22

SUMMER

Lake Champlain Discovery Festival
    (Burlington, VT) 23
Music Mountain Chamber Music Festival (Falls
    Village, CT) 23
Egg Festival (Pittsfield, ME) 24
Pilgrim Wedding (Plymouth, MA) 24
Vermont Quilt Festival (Northfield, VT) 24
Deering Oaks Family Festival (Portland, ME) 25
Vermont Mozart Festival (Brunswick, ME) 25
The Maine Festival (Brunswick, ME) 26
Mystic Outdoor Arts Festival (Mystic, CT) 26

AUTUMN

Massachusetts Cranberry Festival
    (South Carver, MA) 27
Johnny Cake Festival (Usquepaugh,
    West Kingston, RI) 27

Mid-Atlantic Celebrations

WINTER

Festival of Lights (Niagara Falls, NY) 33
Christmas Madrigal Feast (Emmitsburg, MD) 33

Mummers Parade (Philadelphia, PA) 34
Great American Chocolate Festival
    (Hershey, PA) 34
Winter Carnival (Saranec Lake, NY) 35

SPRING

Black Arts Festival (Carlisle, PA) 36
Maple Syrup Demonstration (Thurmont, MD) . . . 36
Wings & Things (Suitland, MD) 36
Cherry Blossom Festival (Washington DC) 37
Apple Blossom Festival (Gettysburg, PA) 37
White Marlin Band Festival Boardwalk Parade
    (Ocean City, MD) 38
Northern Appalachian Festival (Bedford, PA) 38
Annapolis Arts Festival (Annapolis, MD) 39

SUMMER

The Met in The Parks (New York, NY) 40
Kool Jazz Festival (New York, NY) 40
Chautauqua Institution (Chatauqua, NY) 40
Harlem Week (New York, NY) 41

AUTUMN

New York City Street Fairs (New York, NY) 42
Seafood Festival (Hempstead, NY) 43
Wildfowl Carving (Salisbury, MD) 43
The Autumn Leaf Festival (Clarion, PA) 44
Fall Folk Festival (Fulton Co., PA) 44
Village Hallowe'en Parade (Greenwich Village,
    New York) 45

Southern Celebrations

WINTER

Old Salem Christmas (Winston-Salem, NC) 51
Christmas Island (Jekyll Island, GA) 51
Reelfoot Eagle Tours (Reelfoot Lake, TN) 52

Eagles Et Cetera (Bismarck, AR) 52
Old Island Days (Key West, FL) 53
Mardi Gras (New Orleans, LA) 53

SPRING

Peanut Frolic (Tifton, GA) 55
Blowing Rock Annual Opening Day Trout Derby
    (Blowing Rock, NC) 55
Easter Festival (St. Augustine, FL) 55
Shenandoah Apple Blossom Festival
    (Winchester, VA) 56
Birmingham Festival of Arts
    (Birmingham, AL) 57
New Orleans Jazz & Heritage Festival
    (New Orleans, LA) 57
Ramp Festival (Cosby, TN) 58
International Strange Music Weekend (Carter Caves
    State Park, KY) 58
Memphis in May (Memphis, TN) 59
Shrimp Festival (Fernandina Beach, FL) 59
Wodchopping Festival (Webster Springs, WV) . . . 60

SUMMER

Billy Bowlegs Festival (Fort Walton Beach, FL) . . . 60
Hillbilly Day (Mountain Rest, SC) 61
Chincoteague Annual Carnival and Pony Penning
    (Chincoteague, VA) 61
Appalachian Arts & Crafts Festival
    (Beckley, WV) 62
Strange Seafood Exhibition (Beaufort, NC) 62

AUTUMN

Louisiana Shrimp & Petroleum Festival (Morgan
    City, LA) 63
Festivals Acadiens (Lafayette, LA) 63
Corn Island Storytelling Festival
    (Louisville, KY) 64
Louisiana Sugar Cane Festival
    (New Iberia, LA) 65
National Storytelling Festival
    (Jonesborough, TN) 65
Gumbo Festival (Bridge City, LA) 66
Tennessee Valley Old Time Fiddlers Convention
    (Athens, AL) 66
War Eagle Fair (Hindsville, AR) 67

Perryville Battlefield Celebration & Re-Enactment
    (Perryville, KY) 67
Fall Chrysanthemum Extravaganza
    (Theodore, AL) 68

Midwest Celebrations

WINTER

Winter Festival (Omaha, NE) 73
Lakeside Winter Celebration (Fond du
    Lac, WI) 73
Winter Skin Carnaval (Mansfield, OH) 74

SPRING

Kalamazoo Bach Festival (Kalamazoo, MI) 74
Ethnic Festivals (Detroit, MI) 75
International Chicken Flying Meet
    (Rio Grande, OH) 75
St. Louis Storytelling Festival (St. Louis, MO) 76
Eagle Creek Rendezvous (Shakopee, MI) 76

SUMMER

A Taste of Bloomington (Bloomington, IN) 77
International Festival of the Arts (International
    Peace Garden, ND, & Manitoba, Canada) 77
International Freedom Festival (Detroit, MI,
    & Windsor, Ontario) 78
Independence Day (Noblesville, IN) 79
Tom Sawyer Days (Hannibal, MO) 79
Nordic Fest (Decorah, IA) 79
Wheels, Wings & Water Festival
    (St. Cloud, MN) 80
Festa Italiana (Milwaukee, WI) 80
Sinclair Lewis Days (Sauk Centre, MN) 81
Douglas County Historical Steam Festival
    (Arcola, IL) 81
Minneapolis Aquatennial (Minneapolis, MN) 82
Old-Fashioned Threshing Show & Antique Display
    (Freeport, IL) 83
Ozark Empire Fair (Springfield, MO) 83
Coshocton Canal Festival (Van Buren, IN) 83
National Hobo Convention (Britt, IA) 84
Popcorn Festival (Van Buren, IN) 84
Village Art Festival (Nappanee, IN) 84

Oahe Days (Pierre, SD) .85
Minnesota Renaissance Festival
    (Shakopee, MN) 85
Balloon Races (Coshocton, OH) 86

AUTUMN

Santa-Cali-Gon Days (Independence, MO) 86
Hog Capital of the World Festival
    (Kewanee, IL) 87
Fall Festival (Canaan, IN) 87
Popcorn Festival (Valparaiso, IN) 88
Cedarburg Wine & Harvest Festival
    (Cedarburg, WI) 88
Johnny Appleseed Anniversary Festival
    (Fort Wayne, IN) 89
King Turkey Day (Worthington, MN) 89
Octoberfest-Zinzinnati (Cincinnati, OH) 90
Cheese Days (Monroe, WI) 90
Paul Bunyan Show (Nelsonville, OH) 91
Covered Bridge Festival (Madison Co., IA) 91
Feast of the Hunters' Moon (Lafayette, IN) 92
Fall Flyway (Fond du Lac, WI) 92
Autumn on Parade Festival (Oregon, IL) 93
Circleville Pumpkin Show (Circleville, OH) 93

Southwest Celebrations

WINTER

Candlelight Tour of Sam Houston Park
    (Houston, TX) 99
Quartzsite Pow Wow (Quartzsite, AZ) 99
Gold Rush Days (Wickenburg, AZ) 100

SPRING

The Houston Festival (Houston, TX) 101
Tucson Festival (Tucson, AZ) 102
Bird Migration Weekends (Silver City, NM) 102
Fiesta San Antonio (San Antonio, TX) 102
May Fair (McKinney, TX) 103
Rooster Days (Brooken Arrow, OK) 103
Southern Hushpuppy Olympics & Forest Festival
    (Lufkin, TX) 104
Mayfest (Tulsa, OK) 104
Texas Arts & Crafts Fair (Kerrville, TX) 105

SUMMER

Santa Fe Trail Daze (Boise City, OK) 106
New Mexico Arts & Crafts Fair
    (Albuquerque, NM) .106
Taos Chamber Music Festival (Taos, NM) 107
International Brick & Rolling Pin Throw
    (Stroud, OK) 107
Hopi & Navajo Craftsman Exhibitions
    (Flagstaff, AZ) 108
Inter-Tribal Indian Ceremonies (Gallup, NM) . . .108
Texas Folklife Festival (San Antonio, TX) 109
The Great American Duck Race
    (Deming, NM) 109

AUTUMN

Navajo Nation Fair (Window Rock, AZ) 110
Albuquerque International Balloon Fiesta
    (Albuquerque, NM) .110
Helldorado (Tombstone, AZ) 111
Whopping Crane Tours (Rockport, TX) 111
Bat Flight Breakfast (Carlsbad, NM) 112
Will Rogers Day (Claremore, OK) 113

Rocky Mountain Celebrations

WINTER

A Victorian Christmas (Leadville, CO) 119
National Western Stock Show (Denver, CO) 119
Winter Carnival (McCall, ID) 120

SUMMER

National Oldtime Fiddlers' Contest
    (Weiser, ID) 121
Reno Rodeo (Reno, NV) 121
Oro City: Rebirth of a Miner's Camp
    (Leadville, CO) 122
Dixieland Jazz Festival (Sparks, NV) 122
National Basque Festival (Elko, NV) 123
Gift of the Waters (Thermopolis, WY) 123
Art on the Green (Couer d'Alene, ID) 124
Park City Art Festival (Park City, UT) 124
Festival of Nations (Red Lodge, MT) 125

AUTUMN

Wagon Days (Ketchum, ID) 125
International Whistle-Off (Carson City, NV) 126
Great High Sierra Chili Cook-Off
    (Stateline, NV) 126
Harvest Festival (Monte Vista, CO) 127

Pacific Coast

WINTER

Doo Dah Parade (Pasadena, CA) 133
Rose Parade (Pasadena, CA) 134
Winter Carnival (Twin Bridges, CA) 134
Oregon Shakespearean Festival (Ashland, OR) . . 135
Alpenfest (Mt. Shasta, CA) 135
Almond Blossom Festival (Ripon, CA) 136

SPRING

Whale Festivals (Mendocino & Fort
    Bragg, CA) 136
Crabfeed and Auction (Bainbridge
    Island, WA) 137
Apple Blossom Festival (Sebastopol, CA) 137
International Teddy Bear Convention
    (Nevada City, CA) 137
San Francisco International Film Festival (San
    Francisco, CA) 138
Los Angeles Bach Festival (Los Angeles, CA) 138
Cinco de Mayo (San Jose, CA) 139
Irrigation Festival (Sequim, WA) 139
Jumping Frog Jubilee (Angels Camp, CA) 139
Mule Days (Bishop, CA) 140
Renaissance Faires (Agoura & Novato, CA) 140

SUMMER

Flower Festival (Lompoc, CA) 141
Myth California Pageant (San Diego, CA) 142
Summer Solstice Parade (Santa Barbara, CA) 142
Festival of Arts (Laguna Beach, CA) 143
Garlic Festival (Gilroy, CA) 144
Britt Music Festival (Jacksonville, OR) 144
Omak Stampede & Suicide Race (Omak, WA) . . . 145
Steinbeck Festival (Salinas, CA) 145
Old Spanish Days (Santa Barbara, CA) 145

AUTUMN

Bishop Homecoming & Labor Day Rodeo
    (Bishop, CA) 147
Danish Days (Solvang, CA) 147
Wooden Boat Festival (Port Townsend, WA) 148
Pendleton Round-Up (Pendleton, OR) 148
Street Scene Festival (Los Angeles, CA) 149
Monterey Jazz Festival (Monterey, CA) 149
Johnny Appleseed Day (Paradise, CA) 150
Pumpkin Festival (Half Moon Bay, CA) 150
California Wine Festival (Monterey, CA) 151

Hawaii/Alaska/Canada Celebrations

HAWAII

Highland Gathering & Games (Honolulu, HI) . . . 157
Lei Day (Honolulu, HI) 157
Honomu Village Fair (Honomu, HI) 158
Hula Festival (Honolulu, HI) 158
Aloha Week (Honolulu, HI) 158

ALASKA

Anchorage Fur Rendezvous (Anchorage, AK) . . . 159
Winter Carnival (Valdez, AK) 160
Crab Festival (Kodiak, AK) 161
Fourth of July (Seward, AK) 161
Golden Days (Fairbanks, AK) 161
Eagle Council Grounds (Haines, AK) 162

CANADA

Trapper's Festival (The Pas, Manitoba) 162
Festival du Voyageur (Winnipeg, Manitoba) 163
Potato Festivals (Grand Falls & Hartland,
    New Brunswick) 164
Folkfest (Victoria, Brit. Columbia) 164
Klondike Days (Edmonton, Alberta) 165
Seafest (Yarmouth, Nova Scotia) 165
Snowflake Handcraft Fair (North Battleford,
    Saskatchewan) 166

Ethnic Celebrations 167

Native American Celebrations 177

WONDERS AND ASTONISHMENTS
The Why of Celebrations

Holy cow! Run your eye down the Contents list. PEANUT FROLIC. MARDI GRAS. SHENANDOAH APPLE BLOSSOM FESTIVAL. INTERNATIONAL STRANGE MUSIC WEEKEND. CHINCOTEAGUE ANNUAL CARNIVAL AND PONY PEN-NING! (W.C. Fields must've made that one up!) LOUISIANA SHRIMP AND PETROLEUM FESTIVAL. FALL CHRYSANTHEMUM EXTRAVAGANZA! WINTER CARNIVAL. SNOWFLAKE HANDCRAFT FAIR. AUTUMN LEAF, BALLOON, and JUMPING FROG JUBILEES. Don't it make your juices run and your feet want to dust in the GREAT AMERICAN DUCK RACE? Mine do.

But still...

Why am *I* up front here, beating the sideshow banners with my cane, promoting the fevers and grand high dudgeons of it all?

Because, simply, I am a child of festivals, carnivals, sorcerers (real and pretend), and all of the holidays which induce or propel men and women and children to be sublimely foolish for what seems to be no reason at all.

The merest pretext, of course, can cause celebration. Once seized on, the celebration may go on for centuries. One day a year, of course.

All holidays were a special magic to me, as they must be to all children, though we forget to articulate their impact in later years.

I wept every year when Christmas stopped.

I cried every year when Easter Egg hunts were over.

I flooded my cheeks with tears when Halloween came to an end with the charred smell of candle pumpkins and papier mache masks that smothered you with your own hot breath.

I remember the last Fourth of July of my Grandpa's life when I stood on the lawn at midnight after we shot off one hundred dollars worth of fireworks. One hundred dollars, *think* of it! 1925, the year. And five bucks from each aunt, uncle, cousin, grandma, grandpa, mother, father, mobbed on the front porch with their faces tilted to the stars for the next explosion, like two dozen posers waiting for their picture to be taken by a cannon-loaded flash photographer, and there we were and the evening over and myself five and Grandpa lighting the straw in the little tin cup under the last fire balloon, all red-white-and-blue flimsy tissue, an angel's breath, a gentle illumination, held between us like a July prayer, and then we, my Grandpa and I, gave it permission, touched it to heaven, and let it go, drifting up like a soft cry of joy, lighting our faces with angel light, into the stars, away and away, and it was all of life, all of our lives, taken away, never to return, fading, fading.

And I stood on the lawn by my Grandpa, and wept. For even that young, I sensed, I smelled, I knew that it was somehow a symbol of our fragile existence, that it was fire amidst cold, light amidst dark, life amidst death. I had no way to speak those truths. I would find sense and words later. But then, aged five, with my small fiber and my clear eyes, I was shaken by a truth so large I had no way to express it, save with the tears that spilled from my eyelids and dripped off my nose.

Within a year, my Grandfather was dead.

And seeing him in the coffin and lowered in the grave, I knew what Fourth of July, Halloween, Christmas, Easter, and all festivals and celebrations were about.

Very simply, years later, I knew that each one said life and light, while the competition of night moved in to try to snuff the candle and rain on the parade.

Our celebrations are lessons that must be taught again and again, and are often forgotten. Give me, if only for a moment, a parade down a boulevard, a champagne fete in the midst of masks, a superb fireworks war in the sky as I wonder at the incredible beauty of having been alive just this once amidst the long nights and splendid days of time.

The peculiar thing about festivals and celebrations, of course, is that before they begin you often say: Why bother? and when they end you ask: What in hell was *that* all about?

But once they have started and once they are in full feather-fling and eruption, what a lark!

And in the midst of that centrifuge, explosion, and flight, what does it all mean?

Like all acts of creation, whether it is acting, writing, painting, adding sums, delving history, touching bodies, the festival, the carnival says:

Live.

Live today, tonight, this hour.

For tomorrow, who knows?

Put on the mask. Wear the big shoes. March in the mad parade. Give the Christmas gift. Find the Easter Egg. Flower the graveyard dead. Fire the Fourth's full skies. Put up all flags. Remember the dead. Love the living. Watch the dandelion fireworks blossom the heavens and seed the dark. And, in the end, full of festive celebrations, very much love being alive once, never to come back, alive once and full of fire, blood, dream and being.

And name yourself Lucky amidst all the shouts and storms of delight. You live on this day, you march in this parade, you rise in that fire balloon. Glory! Oh, yes, glory! What more can you ask?

From high in your balloon, out in a concourse of canoes, hopping with your Calaveras frogs, or high atop your New Orleans orgy-float cry: "Looky us! Ain't we something!?"

—R.B.

On a Special Day in February 1986

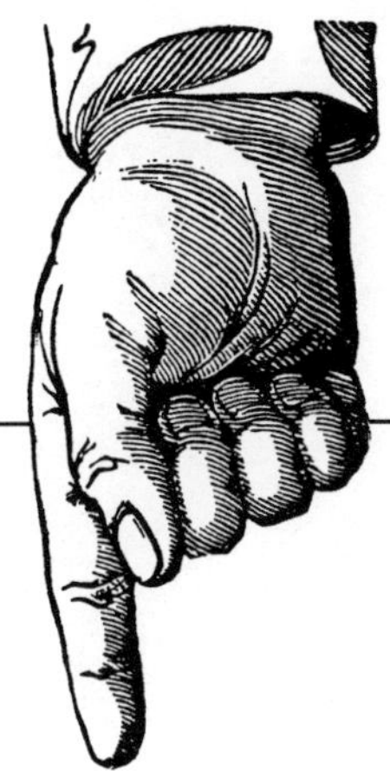

How to Use This Book

You're going to have fun. Furthermore, you'll get an eyeful of some of the most colorful, jubilant, historical, and zany celebrations America has to offer. This book is enlightening for the whole family.

We have divided the country into eight sections and each of these into the four seasons so that wherever you are, whatever the season, you can find some kind of celebration or festival nearby. We have designed section maps (including Hawaii, Alaska, and Canada) to show you locations of all the events and major cities.

In the back of the book you will find a state-by-state directory of Ethnic Celebrations—everything from Thai to German to Scottish to Greek, et al—plus a directory of Native American festivals.

Browse through the Table of Contents to see what's in store for you. With CELEBRATIONS in hand, any vacation can become an adventure to remember.

—The Editors

New England

MAINE
Bangor
Kingfield
Pittsfield
Rangeley
Augusta
St. Albans
Brunswick
Boothbay Harbor
Burlington
Montpelier
NH
Portland
Northfield
Hanover
VT
Concord
Manchester
Boston
MASS
Plymouth
Old Sturbridge Village
South Carver
Falls Village
CONN
RI
Warwick
Mystic
Usquepaugh,
West Kingston

Tug-of-War contestant, Fisherman's Festival.

Annual Samuel de Champlain International Sailboat Race.

Pilgrim wedding ceremony.

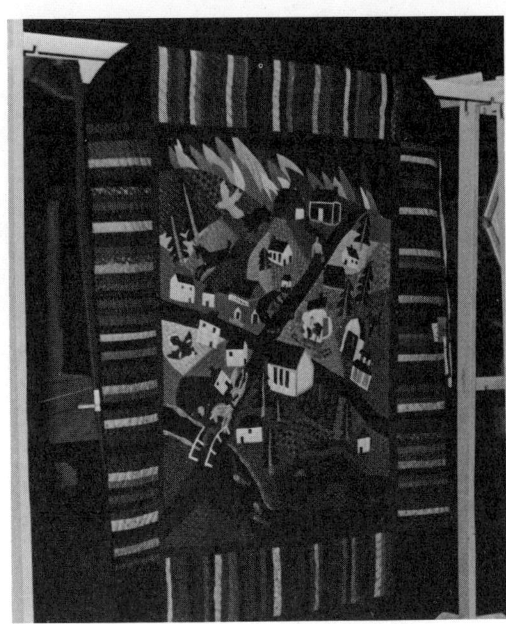

Vermont Quilt Festival.

Dartmouth Winter Carnival ski competition.

JANUARY. 2 days

Snodeo

Rangeley, Maine

Admission charged to some events
Contact: Chamber of Commerce, P.O. Box 317, Rangeley, ME
04970

What is a Snodeo? A rodeo on snowmobiles instead of horses. At least that's how it's done in Maine. The energetic citizens of Maine leave their fireside rocking chairs this weekend to enjoy some lively fun in the winter weather. Events in the Snodeo include a speed race across Rangeley Lake, blindfolded obstacle races where the driver must maneuver along a twisting course following the directions of his partner, a double bag race and the World Snow Golf Championships. Snowmobiles are also on display and demonstration rides are offered. Ice skating is held all day, and on Saturday a big, costumed ice skating party occurs. A snowmobile parade down Main Street is followed by a fireworks display. That same evening brings a party with a lifesize 'Polaris' cake and hot cocoa around the bonfire. Various local establishments provide live entertainment. The weekend concludes with the awards ceremony and a speech by a dignitary from the Maine legislature.

JANUARY. 1 week

White, White World

Sugarloaf, Kingfield, Maine

Admission charged
Contact: Sugarloaf/USA, News Bureau, Carrabassett Valley,
Kingfield, ME 04947

Sugarloaf is over 4,000 feet tall, a big mountain with a week-long festival to celebrate the ski season. Events include a 15k Nordic ski race, a telemark race and a variety of fun races. The Body Sliding Championships feature entrants sliding down the snowy hills on such conveyances as trays or garbage bags. The Silly Slalom is an obstacle course requiring racers to stop and eat cake, ski under obstacles and

perform stunts before reaching the finish line. A King and Queen are chosen and presented at a Coronation Ball. In the evening, various restaurants present special parties including a Kentucky Derby Night. Western Night and a Pajama Party.

Dartmouth Winter Carnival

Hanover, New Hampshire

Admission charged to some events
Contact: New Hampshire Office of Vacation Travel, P.O. Box
856, Concord, NH 03301

College campuses can be pretty dull in winter, but not at Dartmouth where its snow-bound quarter is livened by a grand Winter Carnival. America's oldest and best known collegiate winter weekend is full of activities including such sporting events as inter-collegiate skiing competitions, a figure skating show and snowshoe races. Visitors pose for photos in front of towering snow sculptures, some humorous, others formidable. The evenings bring concerts of jazz or big band music in the famed Hopkins Center on the campus.

❁ *SPRING* ❁

MARCH OR APRIL. 3 days

Fishermen's Festival

Boothbay Harbor, Maine

Admission charged to some events
Contact: Fishermen's Memorial Fund, Box 304, Boothbay
Harbor, ME 04538

Relay racers don't have an easy course in Boothbay Harbor. They are required to run the race holding a codfish while wearing oilskins and hip boots. Not only that, they also must change this attire three

times without losing hold of the fish. This festival features many contests for local fisherfolk and honors those who lost their lives at sea. Since the first festival in 1974, the profits have been set aside to build a memorial honoring fisherman. Built in 1983, a bronze dory rests in a small park overlooking the harbor. The festival continues as fishermen battle it out in a tug-of-war, compete in lobstermen's trap hauling contests, and fight for the championship in shrimp picking, clam and scallop shucking, fish filleting, net mending and lobster picking and eating contests. A Shrimp Princess is crowned and a Cabaret Dance is held. With appetites awakened by the sight of all this seafood, celebrants can attend a fish chowder luncheon or various fish suppers at local churches. The final event of the weekend is a Tall Tales Contest, for adults only, where fishermen exercise their fabled storytelling abilities.

APRIL. 3 days

Vermont Maple Festival

St. Albans, Vermont

Most events free
Contact: Vermont Maple Festival, Box 255, St. Albans, VT
 05478

Maple sugar on snow, maple cotton candy, fried bread dough dripping in Vermont maple syrup, maple fudge, maple cream on a doughnut, maple coffee and maple milkshakes! Almost every maple confection is on hand during Vermont's Maple Festival. You can taste this local syrup at the annual Pancake Breakfast and at the Maple Supper. Amateur chefs compete in

the Maple Cooking Contest, incorporating this essential ingredient in everything from pastries to main entrees. Concessionaires downtown sell maple treats. You can stop at Maple Hall to see how maple syrup is made and view entries in the nine maple categories. This celebration also includes an arts and crafts show and sale, youth talent show, a fiddlers' show and an antique sale. Saturday afternoon brings out the he-men and she-women to compete in such lumberjack events as log chopping, chainsaw contests and log rolling. The final event of this weekend is the grand parade full of bands, floats, queens, horses, clowns and cartoon characters.

MAY. 3 days

Gaspee Days

Warwick, Rhode Island

Free
Contact: Gaspee Day Committee, P.O. Box 1772, Pilgrim
 Station, Warwick, RI 02888

In 1772, H.M.S. *Gaspee* ran aground on a sandbar while harassing a colonist ship suspected of not paying the royal taxes. Unable to leave the sandbar and awaiting the next flood tide, the Captain and crew of the *Gaspee* were surprised by townsfolk from Providence. These patriots captured the men aboard and set the stranded ship afire, the first armed conflict in the Revolutionary War. Rhode Islanders continue to celebrate this 'first blow for freedom' every spring. Warwick holds an arts and crafts festival, a children's colonial costume contest and a big parade. Parade entrants include many colorful floats and dozens of colonial militia units. The look and sounds of the 1700's come alive as costumed marchers simulate fife and drum corps, drum and bugle corps, marching units, minutemen and other regulars of the colonial and crown's military. A costume ball is held. For the dramatic finale of the celebration, a replica of the *Gaspee* is again burned.

MAY/JUNE. 9 days

Wool Days

Old Sturbridge Village, Massachusetts

Admission charged
Contact: Old Sturbridge Village, MA 01566

By 1830, New England could boast of over 1,000 towns. The heart of most communities was the village center where most homes, shops, businesses and meeting halls were located. Surrounding this were farms and, usually, a mill. Old Sturbridge Village is a living museum, a re-creation of a New England town with more than 40 original antique buildings collected from all over the Northwest. Staffed with historically costumed men and women, they go about the daily business of life in the early 19th century.

In the spring, the farmers of Sturbridge shear their sheep and process the wool. In the 1830's most of the wool would have been sold to textile mills, and just enough kept to be woven into warm garments for the farmers' families. You can witness the whole process in late May and early June. First, the sheep are washed in the stream below the farm. Once they are clean, and the farmers are dry, the wool is sheared with hand clippers. Next it is scoured, sorted and dyed. Wool carding, spinning and weaving are exhibited every day. These and many other historically accurate re-creations of 19th century life are conducted in the Museum village year-round. You can wander through the whole town, talk to the staff, watch the demonstrations and special exhibits and photograph the village. Cafeteria, tavern and tap room are open daily, as well as several snack bars and the village bakery with its freshly baked cookies.

☀ *SUMMER* ☀

JUNE 1 THROUGH JULY 4. 1 month

Lake Champlain
Discovery Festival

Burlington, Vermont.

Admission charged to some events
Contact: Chamber of Commerce, 209 Battery St., P.O.
Box 453, Burlington, VA 05402

A month of 'fundays' commemorates the discovery of Lake Champlain on July 4, 1609, by a French adventurer and explorer. Today Samuel de Champlain is less known than the Lake he discovered, although his killing of an Iroquois chief so angered that Indian nation they later allied with the English, perhaps leading to an English-speaking United States rather than a French-speaking country. On the first of June each year, Champlain's discovery is re-enacted in the opening ceremonies. The busy month continues with a hot air balloon festival, boat cruises of the lake, dinner/dance cruises, an international fishing derby with $100,000 in prizes, sailboat races and a floating parade, a clambake, a Shakespeare festival, bird-watching cruises, baseball games and an antique show. Many events appeal to children and include a free ice cream day, tours of a working farm, a strawberry festival and, the most dramatic of all, a big fireworks show over the lake.

JUNE THROUGH SEPTEMBER. 16 concerts

Music Mountain
Chamber Music Festival

Falls Village, Connecticut

Admission charged
Contact: Music Mountain Inc., Box 671, Salisbury, CT 06068

The rolling hills and moss-rimmed streams of the Berkshire Mountains present the perfect setting for this summer chamber music festival. Founded in 1930, Music Mountain is the oldest summer chamber music center in America and now maintains the Manhattan String Quartet as resident artists. They and guest artists perform concerts all summer. Music lovers picnic on the wooded acres of Music Mountain before attending a concert. The music ranges from great masters to contemporary compositions. This festival is small, serious and unpretentious; many members of the audience attend all season long. Music Mountain also sponsors an adult chamber music conference and conducts a teaching seminar for young professionals.

The Manhattan String Quartet in residence at Music Mountain.

Egg Festival

Pittsfield, Maine

Free
Contact: Central Maine Egg Festival, Pittsfield, ME 04967

Some of the most charming celebrations are the small, family-oriented events that bring a whole community together. The Egg Festival has remained non-commercial with plenty of highlights for the youngsters. Downtown features a window painting contest with children creating murals, most of them with a chickeny-type theme. There is also a special children's parade. You don't have to hunt far to find eggs this weekend: decorated ones have their own contest, the World's Largest Egg is judged, eggs are broken for the Omelette Lunch, eggs are dropped from great heights in another contest and the kids have an Egglympics filled with egg games. An Egg Queen is crowned and marches along with other entrants in the big Saturday parade. The sources of all these eggs aren't ignored either. Chickens have their own flying races, and the firemen hold a big chicken barbecue. The weekend offers plenty of music, and closes Saturday night with a big fireworks display.

JULY. 1 day

Pilgrim Wedding

Plimoth Plantation, Plymouth, Massachusetts

Admission charged
Contact: Plimoth Plantation, P.O. Box 1620, Plymouth, MA 02360

Garlanded with rosemary for faithfulness, sage for longevity and marjoram for grace, the 17th century bride goes to meet her groom in splendid Pilgrim attire. Plimoth Plantation, a living museum of the 1600's in Massachusetts, annually presents a country wedding. Re-enacted with careful attention to every detail, the bride and groom are married by Myles Standish and then proceed to a wedding feast where well-wishers and villagers sing rounds of songs, stage games and contests and salute the happiness of the young couple. After the banquet bride and groom are accompanied by friends to their bed chamber where they are joyfully saluted and given a spiced drink of sherry and cream. Every detail of the day's festivities has been carefully researched and costumed staff members faithfully act out the scenario. Visitors to the plantation can view the whole event and join in singing and games. Plimoth Plantation is a replica of a Pilgrim village and Indian campsite of 1627. It includes a full-scale copy of the *Mayflower.* Here visitors can see what life was like for the colonists over 300 years ago.

JULY. 3 days

Vermont Quilt Festival

Northfield, Vermont

Admission charged
Contact: Mary K. Ryan, Grandview Terrace, Rutland, VT 05701

Old quilters never die, they just go to pieces. And, their piecework can be viewed in Vermont every summer. Quilting is an American art form born of necessity, when pioneer women had to make warm bedcovers from fabric scraps. Transmitting need into art, they crafted their beautiful and sophisticated patterns. Recently, quilt making has experienced a

resurgence of interest as women's work is being studied and old crafts are again being practised. At the Vermont Festival both antique and contemporary quilts can be viewed. A juried quilt contest features contestants from many countries. Expert and professional quilters show their work. Miniatures are displayed and special vignettes show quilts in authentic antique settings. The craftsperson can attend various classes, workshops and lectures as well as two banquets. An appraisal service is held for the evaluation of antique quilts.

JULY, 1 week

Deering Oaks Family Festival

Portland, Maine

Free admission
Contact Chamber of Commerce, 142 Free Street, Portland,
ME 04101

One of Maine's premier attractions, the Deering Oaks celebration knows the way to a festival-goer's heart is through his stomach. Tantalizing choices are offered by many local restaurants at their "Taste of Greater Portland' event. And 27 non-profit organizations set up food booths to sell everything from fried clams, crab rolls and lobster to strawberry shortcake and fudge. With your stomach full, you can drop the kids off at one of the children's workshops and proceed to a jazz concert, theater performance, storyteller event, vaudeville show, rock concert, or an assortment of specialty acts like a clown show or unicyclist act. On Friday evening, a big parade marches past the Duck Pond and through Deering Oaks Park. In keeping with the traditions of family fun, this festival sponsors several 'funny' races, including underwater heats for local lobsters and a Wine Race with competitors making their way through an obstacle course while balancing a tray loaded with full wine glasses. One of the most popular attractions is the big fireworks display set off on Saturday evening. Each year the fifty acres of spacious Deering Oak Park are crowded with families enjoying all the food and fun of this celebration.

JULY/AUGUST. 3 weeks

Vermont Mozart Festival

Burlington, Vermont

Admission charged
Contact: Vermont Mozart Festival, P.O. Box 512, Burlington,
VT 05402

Despite its title, Mozart isn't the only composer performed at the thirteen concerts of this summer

A magnificent estate provides a beautiful background for an evening concert.

music celebration. The professional artists and ensembles present works of many other classical composers as well. Concerts occur at a variety of evocative settings including a cathedral in Burlington, the coach yard of a large estate, various recital halls and resorts, an opera house and even during an evening ferry cruise. The artists vary from year to year, and they teach student workshops as well as concertize.

Comedy abounds at the Festival. Here a fast-talking 'pitchman' draws a crowd.

AUGUST. 3 days

The Maine Festival

Bowdoin College, Brunswick, Maine.

Admission charged
Contact: The Maine Festival, P.O. Box 192, Brunswick, Maine 04011

A roistering combination of avant garde and traditional, the Maine Festival annually brings together a diverse group of artists, residents and visitors. Conceived of as a 'cultural jam session,' this festival is characterized by the tremendous variety of its arts events. Where else would contemporary improvisational theatre, fusion jazz and rock'n roll drama perform alongside woodcarvers, quilt makers, rug hookers, storytellers and fiddlers? Six hundred artists participate or display their work this weekend. Friday is children's day with a reduced fare. Outdoor sculpture, an invitational art exhibit, a photography exhibit, crafts displays and film showings accompany live performances. Tantalizing foods are offered to keep everyone adequately fueled.

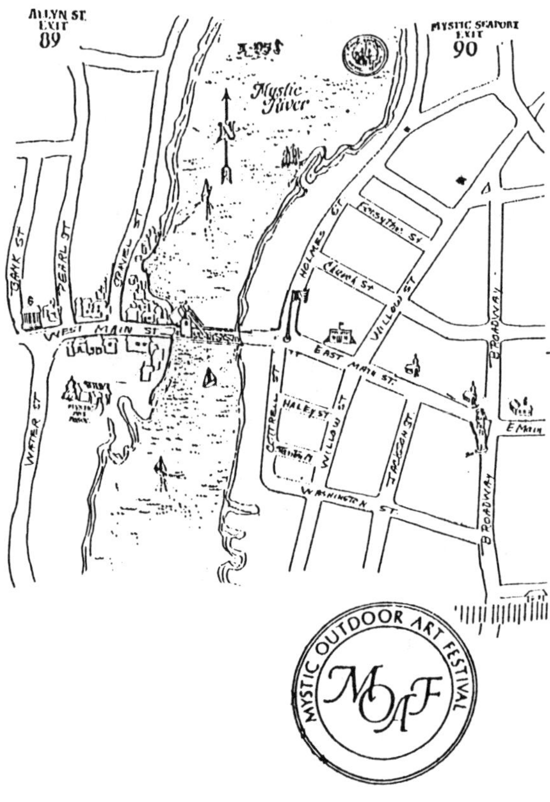

AUGUST. 2 days

Mystic Outdoor Arts Festival

Mystic, Connecticut

Free
Contact: Chamber of Commerce, Box 143, Mystic, CT 06355

The East's most widely known sidewalk art show, MOAF turns Mystic's Main Street into a mile-long art gallery and spills over onto half a dozen side streets along the way. Mystic is a historic seaport village that retains much of the charm of the 18th century in its architecture and ambience. Artists from all over the East vie for exhibit space this weekend. Limited to 400, and rigorously juried, the event attracts exhibitors in almost every medium. Almost 100,000 visitors come to stroll through the stalls, many buy, bargain or barter for the art. Browsers also enjoy a walking tour of the historic homes of Old Mystic.

SEPTEMBER/OCTOBER. 4 days

Massachusetts Cranberry Festival

Edaville Railroad, South Carver, Massachusetts

Admission charged
Contact: Massachusetts Cranberry Festival, P.O. Box 7, South Carver, MA 02366

During harvest, the flooded cranberry bogs are completely covered with buoyant red berries and resemble red seas. Edaville Railroad is a family theme park located on a cranberry plantation, and features a small gauge railroad which completely circles the facilities. Each fall, the berries (America's favorite native fruit) are harvested and the visitor can ride the train and watch the fruit being scooped up. The festival includes an annual loggers' and woodsmen's competition, a 4H fair, a cranberry quilt display, a juried crafts show and cranberry cookery demonstrations and contests. The Edaville Railroad features a museum of New England heritage, a half-scale model of a 19th century New England village, a petting zoo and a tempting barbecue chicken pavilion.

OCTOBER. 2 days

Johnny Cake Festival

Usquepaugh, West Kingston, Rhode Island

Free
Contact: Kenyon Corn Meal, Co., P.O. Box 221, Usquepaugh, West Kingston, RI 02892

The flour mill in Usquepaugh was built a hundred years ago and overlooks the waterfall below the mill pond on the Queen's River. A small, village fair is held here each year to celebrate the Johnny Cake and the rural life it represents in Rhode island. Daily tours of the grist mills are conducted and the gift shop sells its products as well as a wide variety of toys and kitchen items. Other native foods of the area are featured too, including clam cakes, chowder and other homebaked goods. Early American home construction is demonstrated and local and antique crafts are shown. A big parade is held on Sunday with bands, color guards, fire equipment, antique automobiles, scouts and local dignitaries. Chefs demonstrate Johnny Cake cookery with wit and wisdom in the millyard. Children are not forgotten, either. Special games and face painting entertain the youngsters. The local Narragansett Indians demonstrate their tribal dances and are celebrated as the originators of the Johnny Cake.

Mid-Atlantic

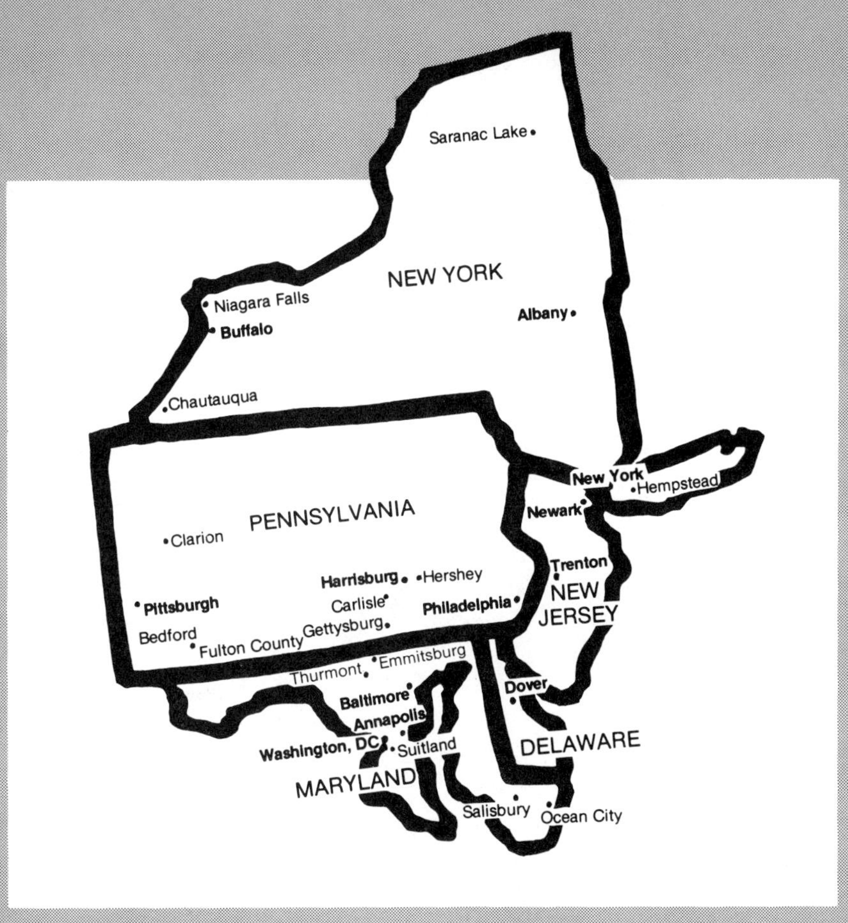

New York City Street Fair.

Apple Butter Boil at the Fall Folk Festival.

Oldtimers Parade in Fulton County, Pennsylvania.

White Marlin Band Festival Boardwalk Parade.

Ballet performance at the Chautauqua Institution.

LATE NOVEMBER THROUGH EARLY JANUARY. 6 weeks

Festival of Lights

Niagara Falls, New York

Free exhibits, admission charged to musical and theatrical events

Contact: Niagara Falls Convention Bureau, 300 4th St., Niagara Falls, NY 14303

Tens of thousands of twinkling lights glitter in downtown Niagara Falls during the holiday season. A five-block area of the city, near the thundering falls, is transformed into a winter fantasyland. Dozens of huge storybook paintings decorate the area, their brilliant characters welcoming the visitor. Inside the Convention Center and the various plazas and malls of the area, large animated attractions delight the viewer with such scenes as a Victorian Christmas, the Gingerbread House, the Christmas Circus, the Rainbow Village, the Three Little Pigs Village and the Ice Castle. The jewel of the festival is the Wintergarden, a ten-story indoor botanical garden filled with lush tropical plants decorated for the season. Throughout the festival, the Convention Center hosts a large variety of live entertainment and the Wintergarden offers free nightly concerts.

EARLY DECEMBER. 3 DAYS

Christmas Madrigal Feast

Mount Saint Mary's College, Emmitsburg, Maryland

Admission charged.

Contact: Rev. Dr. David W. Shaum, Mount Saint Mary's College, Emmitsburg, MD 21727

Enjoy a festive dinner while the Mount Saint Mary's singers perform their Christmas program. Themes over the years have included a Victorian Christmas, an Edwardian Christmas, a medieval Christmas in Camelot, a pioneer holiday in old Williamsburg, Christmas in Santa's toy shop and an Austrian Christmas. The beautifully costumed singers perform traditional choral music and the Mount Saint Mary's food service caters the meal. Word of this celebration has spread far and wide, each performance sells out and tickets should be requested early in the month. Many faithful supporters return year after year.

Mummers Parade

Philadelphia, Pennsylvania

Free
Contact: Department of Recreation, 1470 Municipal Services
Building, Philadelphia, PA 119102

According to the dictionary, 'mummers' are costumed merrymakers parading in a festival, but this simple description hardly covers the annual spectacle in Philadelphia. World famous, the Mummers Parade ushers in the new year and is probably the longest parade in the world. The 1985 parade took twelve hours to pass the judge's stand! Ancient in origin, perhaps dating back to medieval France, the Mummers compete in four categories: Comic, Fancy, String Band and Brigade. Cash prizes are awarded each year to the winning clubs by the City of Philadelphia. Costumes are enormous, often two or three times the size of the wearer, and constructed of brilliant satins, brocades and lames with glittering sequins, all surrounded by colorfully bobbing feather plumes.

The Mummers are members of private clubs, and take all year to prepare for this one-day event. Each club marches up Broad Street, performing musical selections, dancing, clowning and acting, all to the delight of hundreds of thousands of viewers.

Great American Chocolate Festival

Hershey, Pennsylvania

Admission charged
Contact: Hershey Entertainment and Resort Company,
Corporate Marketing, 400 West Hersheypark Dr.,
Hershey, PA 17033

Chocoholics can rejoice at this festival created just for

them and centering around the most chocolate-laden holiday of the year—Valentine's Day. Hershey, Pennsylvania is home of the grandfather of the American chocolate business, and site of the Hershey Resort Hotel. Each year a nationally known chef is the highlighted speaker and demonstrator. The festival kicks off with a theme party, elaborately decorated and featuring special treats. One year it was a 1950s style party with a soda fountain and do-it-yourself chocolate sundaes. A Chocolate Fashion Show features strolling models showing off the newest in chocolate desserts. You'll find a chocolate auction and a demonstration of chocolate crafts, including a miniature town made out of Hershey bars. Hershey chefs and guest culinary experts show you the intricacies of such delicacies as chocolate ice cream, mousse, pasta and even pizza. Home economists instruct you in how to adapt professional cooking techniques to the home kitchen with such modern appliances as the microwave oven. Meals at the Hershey Hotel emphasize chocolate specialties, and Valentine's Day brings a special dinner and dance. Local contestants enter a chocolate bake-off and everyone can sample the winning creations.

FEBRUARY. 5 days

Winter Carnival

Saranac Lake, New York

Most events are free
Contact: Saranac Lake Area Chamber of Commerce, 30 Main
St., Saranac Lake, NY 12983

A gleaming ice palace is the central attraction of Winter Carnival. Weeks ahead of time, hand-hewn blocks of ice, some weighing 600 pounds, are dragged from the lake and assembled into fanciful architecture. Carnival week features many outdoor sporting events including skiing, skating races, softball-in-the-snow, ice golf, rugby, ice hockey and broom hockey. Two parades are held on Main Street, a grand parade and a costumed children's parade. Indoor types will appreciate the theatrical production and the "Snow Ball." The exciting climax of the festival comes the last night when snowmobilers circle the ice palace, carrying torches in the moonlight to signal the start of an elaborate fireworks display on the shores of the lake.

Black Arts Festival

Dickinson College, Carlisle, Pennsylvania

Admission charged to some events
Contact: Dickinson College, Carlisle, PA 17013

Black culture, history and political impact are celebrated annually at Dickinson College. Themes vary from year to year. The college schedules important speakers, artists, theatrical performances and exhibits that all address Black culture. Some events take place in the classrooms, others are scheduled for larger forums. The Black Arts Festival has been bringing diversity to the college and celebrating this unique American heritage for eighteen years.

MIDDLE TWO WEEKENDS IN MARCH. 4 days

Maple Syrup Demonstration

Cunningham Falls State Park, Thurmont, Maryland

Free
Contact: Cunningham Falls State Park, 14039 Catoctin
Hollow Road, Thurmont, MD 21788

Long before the Pilgrims landed, Indians produced maple syrup and traded it around the East Coast.

One of America's oldest agricultural products, maple syrup is produced in a short season, usually from mid-February through March. Freezing nights followed by warm days are necessary for the sap to rise and fall in hard maple trees. At Cunningham Falls State Park you can view the entire process. Trees are tapped and the sap collected in buckets. Next the sap is boiled in batches until it reaches the right temperature and concentration. Naturalists give talks and show films; and the visitor can sample many different maple products or purchase refreshments, including pancakes and maple syrup!

APRIL. 2 days

Wings & Things

Smithsonian's Paul E. Garber Facility
Suitland, Maryland

Free
Contact: Office of Public Affairs, Smithsonian Institution,
Washington, D.C. 20560

Photograph the kids in leather goggles and an aviator's scarf next to an old propeller-driven stunt

plane. Or pose mom in a jet helmet sitting in the training cockpit of a F-100 Super Sabre. Visitors to the Smithsonian's annual Wings & Things can see antique and historically significant flying machines of all types, from the earliest aircraft to manned space ships. The skilled craftsmen in charge of the restoration of these vehicles will talk to visitors about their work. Model airplane building is also demonstrated, and safe telescope viewing of the sun is provided. During the two-day event, music from U.S. Navy bands resounds in the courtyard. Food and soft drinks are for sale.

APRIL. 1 week

Cherry Blossom Festival

Washington, DC

Most events free
Contact: Convention and Visitors Association, 1575 Eye St.
*   NW, Washington, DC 20005*

Washington's famous cherry trees were a gift in 1912 from the government of Japan. The original suggestion to plant them came from First Lady Mrs. William Howard Taft. Upon hearing of her interest, the Mayor of Tokyo donated more than 3,000 trees raised from cuttings from Tokyo's famous collection of cherries along the Arakawa River. Curiously, the Washington trees were later used to provide plantings to replenish Tokyo's groves in 1952. Seriously neglected during World War II, many of the Japanese trees had died. In 1965, the Japanese made another generous gift of almost 4,000 trees to Washington. All these trees bloom in spring when Washington

holds its famous Cherry Blossom Festival. Scheduled for early April, it usually occurs when the trees are in full flower, decorating the city with millions of pink and white blossoms. A huge parade is held, the largest spectator event in Washington, with bands, floats, the Cherry Blossom Queen and dignitaries aplenty. The festival is opened each year with the lighting of an authentic 17th century stone lantern, another gift from Japan. The lantern is located near the Jefferson Memorial on the Tidal Basin, and the whole area is rimmed with glorious cherry trees.

FIRST FULL WEEKEND IN MAY. 2 days

Apple Blossom Festival

Gettysburg, Pennsylvania

Admission charged to fairground
Contact: Apple Blossom Festival, 33 York St., Gettysburg, PA
*   17325*

By May, the apple, peach and cherry orchards adorning the hills around Gettysburg reach full bloom.

They provide a colorful and fragrant background to the Apple Blossom Festival commemorating the five million bushels of apples shipped from Adams County each year. A Queen is crowned, and the visitor can attend apple pie eating or apple bobbing contests. Fresh apples, apple cider, apple butter and candied apples are sold as well as apple desserts. The highlight of the celebration are tours of the orchards. You can either join a bus tour or stroll through the blossoming trees at your own pace.

baton twirlers and pompom girls from a six-state area. More than 25 bands and 40 floats come down the boardwalk in a stirring succession of music from Sousa to Gershwin with some jazz thrown in. You have your choice of watching from your towel on a white sandy beach or relaxing at an outdoor table on the inland side while the bands pound by on the resonant boardwalk.

MAY. 2 days

Northern Appalachian Festival

Bedford, Pennsylvania

Most events free
Contact: Northern Appalachian Festival, P.O. Box 1771,
Bedford, PA 15522

MID-MAY. 1 day

White Marlin Band Festival Boardwalk Parade

Ocean City, Maryland

Contact: White Marlin Band Festival, 111 Wicomico St.,
Ocean City, MD 21842

The white marlin capital of the world kicks off its summer season on the second Saturday of May with a booming parade of marching bands, majorettes,

Who invented the bed race? The Northern Appalachian Festival asserts its race was the original. The beds are first paraded downtown, then raced pell-mell up the street by teams of pushers while agonized occupants hold on for dear life. Will the antique four-poster out distance the iron cot? Although the bed race is the exciting highlight of this celebration, other events will draw the visitors attention too. Antique autos and collectors' Corvettes are displayed while street rods parade. Firemen vie in battles of barrel, pumping and water relay races.

Many local agencies cooperate on a Health Fair. A potpourri of food booths cater to hungry appetites.

Entertainment includes puppeteers, gospel singers, country bands, bluegrass music, high school bands and performances for the deaf. Fort Bedford Park hosts an encampment of members of the Muzzle Loading Rifle Association with daily demonstrations of such pioneer-day skills as gun smithing, powder horn making, knife and tomahawk throwing. Featured guests are the cheerleaders and mascots from the University of Pittsburgh and Pennsylvania State University.

☀ SUMMER ☀

JUNE. 3 days

Annapolis Arts Festival

Annapolis, Maryland

Admission charged
Contact: Crosby Communications, 1982 Moreland Parkway, Annapolis, MD 21401

Overlooking the harbor, Annapolis' colorful waterfront park is the site of this annual arts festival. Inside huge multi-colored tents, scores of artisans exhibit their skillful creations. Local music, dance, and theatre groups perform on the outdoor stage, and world-renowned headliners appear in the evenings. One unique exhibit is the Discovery Tent, off-bounds to grownups. Here children experience the thrill of creativity and explore art through all their senses. The festival is within walking distance of Annapolis' famous landmarks, and dozens of shops and restaurants.

The Met in the Parks

New York, New York

Free
Contact: Metropolitan Opera Association, Lincoln Center, New York, NY 10023

The Mayor opens this series of free opera concerts in the parks of New York with a proclamation forbidding rain. The first performance, in Central Park, draws at least 75,000 music lovers to hear a full performance of a classic grand opera, complete with world-famous cast. The audience sits on the lawn, some arrive eight hours early to guarantee a good seat, and most people bring a fancy picnic with gourmet wines and festive candles to light the evening. Performed in a portable acoustical shell, the opera is amplified so everyone can hear. From Manhattan, the performances travel to parks in Brooklyn, Queens, the Bronx, Staten Island and Nassau County. These performances are staged more simply than inside a theater, but the music is magnificient and the enormous crowds consider the Met in the Parks the best way to start summer.

END OF JUNE. 10 days

Kool Jazz Festival

New York, New York

Admission charged for all events
Contact: Kool Jazz Festival New York, P.O. Box 1169, Ansonia Station, New York, NY 10023

This ten-day event is undisputedly the greatest jazz festival in the world. Ricocheting around New York City in the summer, the Kool Jazz Festival is the direct descendant of the Newport Jazz Festival.

Featuring concerts and performance all around the city, the program reads like the *Who's Who* of jazz. All the greats perform here and all styles of jazz are played including Dixieland, ragtime, rhythm and blues, modern, pop, fusion and even contemporary classics from Japan, Brazil, India and Africa. In 1982 the festival was expanded to twenty other cities around the United States, bringing world-class headliners to these cities as featured performers and also employing the best among local talent. Kool Jazz Festival New York celebrates America's most unique art form.

END OF JUNE THROUGH AUGUST. 9 weeks

Chautauqua Institution

Chautauqua, New York

Admission charged, varied accomodations available
Contact: Chautauqua Institution, Dept. G, Box 1095, Chautauqua, NY 14722

The century-old Chautauqua Institution is located in a Victorian lakeside village and still carries the charm and ambience of that period. A varied schedule of art, summer. Some visitors come for a weekend, many stay the whole season. Prominent lecturers, authors and politicians speak from the lecture platform. The audience is noted for its sophisticated challenges and questions. The summer school programs covers a wide range of subjects, including mathematics, language, arts and computers.

Chautauqua's grounds are filled with diverse architectural styles, the most predominant being the Victorian style.

Recreational facilites are available for all members of the family—tennis courts, beaches, an 18-hole golf course, hiking, biking and jogging, fishing, boating, windsurfing and sailing on the lake, and a Sports Club with everything from exercise classes to lawn bowling. The Chautauqua Symphony presents 21 concerts while the Opera Company performs major operas with world famous artists. The Acting Company

The 74-member Chatauqua Symphony Orchestra is the heart of Chautauqua.

offers a variety of theatrical performances. You'll find an art gallery where Chautauqua's educational program contributes performers and exhibitors each season. The religious program offers daily services and lectures. Chautauqua's 19th century heritage of personal enrichment thrives in the diversity of its offerings.

EARLY AUGUST. 14 days

Harlem Week

New York, New York

Admission charged to some events
Contact: Harlem Week, 310 Lenox Avenue, Room 305, New York, NY 10027

Harlem is the center of American Black and Hispanic cultures and has acted as a magnet to minority people for over a hundred years. Once visited frequently by other New Yorkers and tourists alike, it has slowly become an area ignored by the rest of the world. Recently, however, many community revitalization efforts have been organized bringing a second renaissance to one of the country's largest ethnic neighborhoods. Harlem Week annually attracts more than a million visitors to its rich variety of performances, street parties, conferences and attractions.

The events are designed to showcase minority and local talent as well as providing residents with a variety of educational opportunities. A Youth Career Conference focuses on the young people of Harlem with panelists discussing job skills and opportunities. The Elder's Jubilee is a tribute to senior citizens and the many older leaders of the community. It includes entertainment and exhibits on everything from fire prevention to money management for seniors. The Economic Development Conference brings business leaders uptown to discuss real estate tips, business management, tax consulting and networking. The Health Care Conference has representatives from local hospitals and clinics as well as medical vans on site for check-ups.

The music and cultural events are the jubilant center of this celebration. Concerts include reggae, calypso, blues, gospel and Latin music. Performers range from local groups to big name headliners. Theatrical performances, a fashion show, church services, a parade and carnival and special art exhibits are all staged this week. Highlighting the whole event is Harlem Day with entertainment, sports demonstrations and hundreds of booths selling ethnic food and arts along 125th Street and 135th Street. With a festival this big, it is no wonder Harlem is now being called 'The Heart and Soul of the Big Apple.'

✳ *AUTUMN* ✳

FALL

New York City Street Fairs

New York, New York

Free
Contact: Conventions and Visitors Bureau, 2 Columbus Circle, New York, NY 10019

To most visitors, New York is a street fair all year round. However, in late summer and early fall the residents take to their streets in an outburst of enthusiasm. Street fairs of all kinds are planned, drawing thousands to sample ethnic foods, enjoy free entertainment, shop for arts and crafts and support civic programs. These events are free and you don't have to be from the neighborhood to enjoy them. The following is a sample of fairs. Check with the Convention and Visitors Bureau for specific dates and times (which may vary yearly).

FEAST OF SAN GENNARO FESTIVAL. Mulberry Street from Columbus Park to Old St. Patrick's Cathedral.

THIRD AVENUE FESTIVAL. Third Avenue from 68th to 90th Street.

WASHINGTON MARKET STREET FAIR. Greenwich Street at Chambers Street.

NEW YORK IS BOOK COUNTRY FAIR. Fifth Avenue from 48th to 57th Street.

ONE WORLD FAIR. Around St. Vartan Cathedral, Second Avenue and 35th Street.

JEWISH PEOPLEHOOD FESTIVAL. West End Avenue from 73rd to 78th Street.

BRAZILIAN FESTIVAL. West 46th St. between Fifth and Sixth Avenue.

THIRD AVENUE MERCHANTS ASSOCIATION FAIR. Third Avenue from 14th to 34th Streets.

AUTUMN CRAFTS FESTIVAL. East 35th Street and Second Avenue.

WASHINGTON SQUARE OUTDOOR ART EXHIBIT. Streets around Washington Square.

STREET FAIR. East 9th Street between First and Second Avenues.

STREET FAIR. West 55th Street between Tenth and Eleventh Avenues.

CENTRAL PARK SOUTH ART EXHIBIT. Avenue of the Americas and 59th Street.

WASHINGTON MARKET STREET FAIR. Greenwich Street at Chambers Street.

SEPTEMBER. 2 days

Seafood Festival

Hempstead, New York

Free
Contact: Department of Industry and Commerce, 350 Front St., Hempstead, NY 11550

Saluting its nautical heritage, the town of Hempstead annually holds its mouthwatering Seafood Festival. Merchants from the area display and sell a delicious variety of seafood, everything from clam chowder, garlic crabs, shrimp pizza, langostinos, seafood salads, mussels, fresh lobsters to scungilli and much more. Between bites, the visitor can witness a multi-hull or sailboard regatta, view the sand-sculpting contest, watch a Queen crowned, listen to jazz or watch a seafood filleting and preparation demonstration. The athletic can enter the biathalon or surf-casting contest. Over 80,000 people attended the event in 1984 and munched their way through tons of seafood.

Depicted in a sand sculpture by Frank Verni of Baldwin are a racing horse and jockey that symbolize the saving of Roosevelt Racetrack.

OCTOBER. 3 days

Wildfowl Carving & Art Exhibition

Salisbury, Maryland

Admission charged
Contact: The Ward Foundation, 655 S. Salisbury Blvd., Salisbury, MD 21801

An elegant but little known art, wildfowl carving was once considered an endangered craft. Now, however, the art is thriving. Originally carved to attract wildfowl within the hunter's range, artists now concentrate on accurately and beautifully recreating the bird and its habitat. The Wildfowl Exhibition in Salisbury annually displays the work of the most

outstanding carvers and painters. A tiny Western Grebe chick peers from underneath its mother's wing, two Red Jungle Fowl fight each other, a hummingbird hovers in front of a red flower, startled bobwhites hide among the cactus. Hours of careful observation in the field must go into every carving.

A public auction and all-you-can-eat seafood festival are also part of the exhibit. You may also want to stop by the North American Wildfowl Art Museum at Salisbury State College where sophisticated displays introduce the viewer to the quiet wetland habitat of the marsh, and the workshop of an industrious carver. Antique hunting decoys and the works of the finest contemporary carvers are on display. The staff conducts tours, and there is a gift shop.

OCTOBER, 1 week

The Autumn Leaf Festival

Clarion, Pennsylvania

Free
Contact: Chamber of Commerce, 517 Main St., Clarion, PA
16214

Nature paints the colorful backdrop for the Autumn Leaf Festival. Held when the fall foliage is at its multi-hued brilliance, this celebration is full of activities. A parade proudly marches down Main Street, Miss Teenage Autumn Leaf is crowned and goes on to compete in other pageants. Sidewalk sales and flea markets abound, arts and crafts are shown and the Jaycees hold a dance. Visitors can ride a fire truck, tour the Historical Museum and view antique motorcars.

A petting zoo and carnival are favorites with the children. And, of course, many tours of the fabulous countryside foliage are scheduled.

THIRD WEEKEND IN OCTOBER, 3 days

Fall Folk Festival

Fulton County, Pennsylvania

Admission charged to fairgrounds
Contact: Fulton County Tourist Promotion Agency, P.O. Box
141, McConnellsburg, PA 17233

Fulton County shows how people used to live on the farms and in the small towns of America. Each fall they bring the past to life with a special festival. Events all over the county recreate the past and keep folk traditions from another era alive. With autumn at its height, visitors can view an Oldtimers Parade, tour historic homes and churches, visit country kitchens, attend an apple butter boil or watch candle dipping. You'll find an arts and crafts show, a huge quilt contest and sale, displays of old-time farm machinery and cars, while a giant Belgian orchestral organ pours forth its music.

OCTOBER 31, 7:00 p.m.

Village Hallowe'en Parade

Greenwich Village: along Sixth Avenue between Houston and 10th Street and ending at Washington Square.

Free.
Contact: Karen Bacon, 349 West End, New York, NY 10014

This has got to be the biggest, wildest and spookiest parade in America, winding through the streets of Greenwich Village on Halloween. Imagine 60,000 participants and a quarter million onlookers! Ralph Lee, director, first brainstormed this event in 1974 and created many of the gigantic and gorgeously grotesque puppets that appear year after year. In addition to ghoulish costumes and certain surprise events that occur—like the vacant building rigged into a haunted house with ghostly sound and lighting effects—you'll be entertained by a happy range of bands, from Samba to Dixieland, jugglers and mimes.

Author Edward Hoagland calls this the New York version of Mardi Gras. In the *New York Times* he wrote: "A friend who danced for two hours through the Village streets in last year's Halloween parade as an orange-coated fox found that, peering through the eyeholes of his muzzly mask, he took a new view of other people and himself.

"It wasn't so much a child's or even a fox's mind that he had as an open mind. That the sexes blended ...goes without saying: bearded brides and burnished slaves, Mona Lisa as a man. But so did species: flying lizards, a five-humped camel, a 12-foot purple centi-pede, and he noticed that among the participants an extraordinary civility obtained.

"Thirteen people carried a 40-foot snake on poles. A Floozie and a Dandy quarreled and quadrilled. Yama the Chinese Lord of Death and Nananan the Irish Sea God rode in chariots. But mummers in blood-and-bones costumes allowed elbow room to birds of paradise and stilt-walkers, and mice and cats performing a nursery tale.

"He noticed that the fantasies didn't necessarily stay what they started out to be. People painted with tears began to smile. Fright wigs became poignant. He did feel foxlike, however. His mask's paint and glue smelled like a true fox's pelt and his black nose, jutting out into the world asking uncommon questions, doubled itself in front of him, being so close to his eyes. Little kids debated what he was—wolf or dog—and he stopped to shake hands when not too enraptured by the oom-pah of the trombones.

"A 20-foot three-masted bark sailed down the street overrun with rats trying to get off. A spider as big as the ship cavorted on top of the Jefferson Market Library."

South

WEST VIRGINIA
Winchester
Cincoteague
Webster Springs
Charleston
VIRGINIA
Beckley
Richmond
Carter Caves
Louisville
Lexington
Perryville
KENTUCKY
Winston-Salem
Greensboro
Raleigh
Jonesborough
Cosby
Blowing Rock
NORTH CAROLINA
Beaufort
Nashville
Knoxville
Reelfoot Lake
TENNESSEE
Charlotte
Hindsville
Memphis
Mountain Rest
ARKANSAS
Columbia
SOUTH CAROLINA
Little Rock
Athens
Bismarck
Atlanta
Charleston
Birmingham
ALABAMA
GEORGIA
MISSISSIPPI
Montgomery
Savannah
Shreveport
Jackson
Tifton
Jekyll Island
LOUISIANA
Theodore
Fernandina Beach
Fort Walton Beach
Tallahassee
Baton Rouge
St. Augustine
Morgan City
New Iberia
Bridge City
New Orleans
Orlando
Tampa
FLORIDA
Miami
Key West

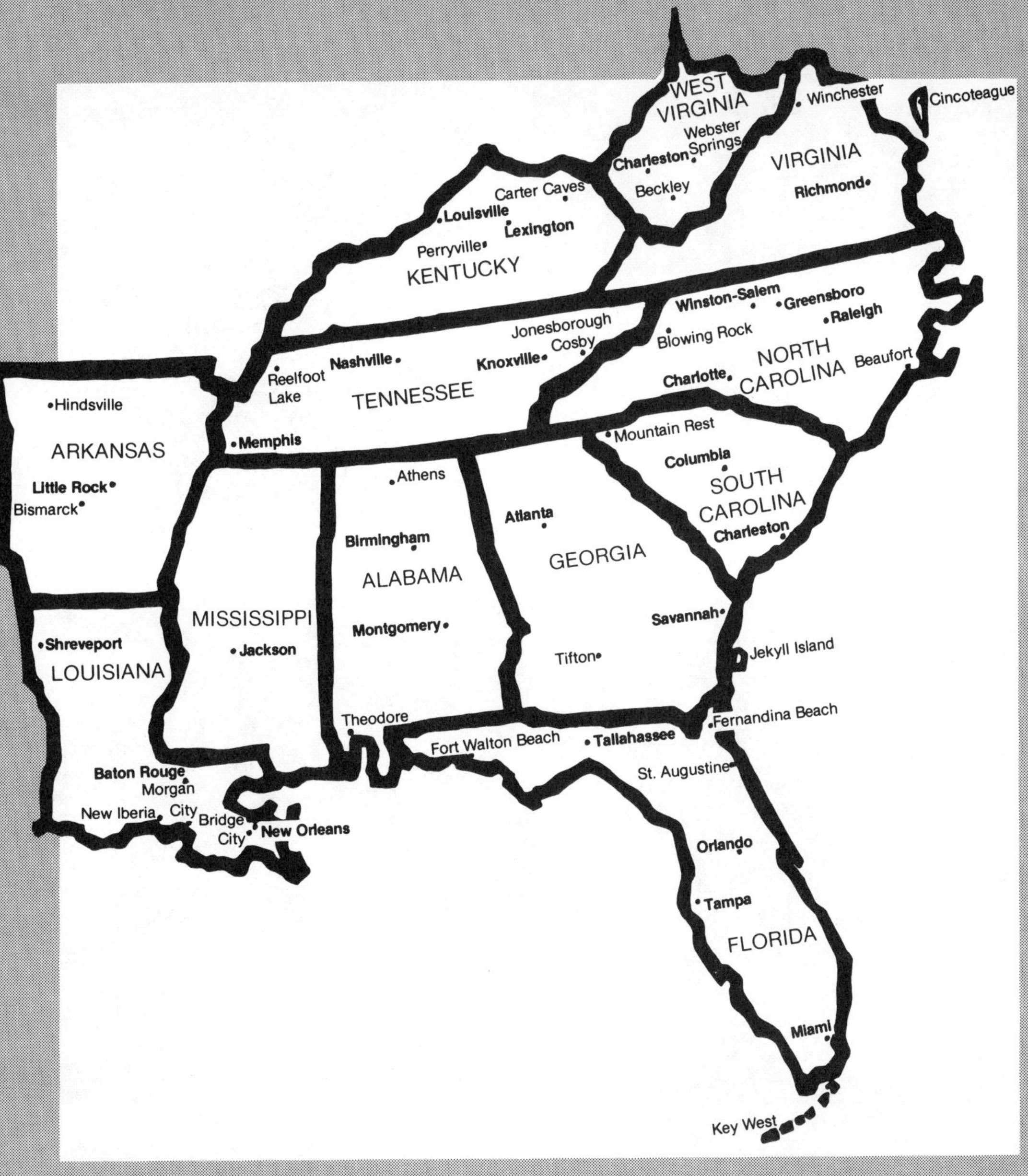

Festivals Acadians

Serving up Triggerfish Chowder at the Strange Seafood Exhibition.

Picking tunes at the Peanut Frolic.

Mardi Gras!

Caroling by the Moravian Band during Old Salem Christmas.

A choral group and a string quartet entertain Old Salem Christmas visitors.

MID-DECEMBER. 2 days

Old Salem Christmas

Winston-Salem, North Carolina

Admission charged
Contact: Old Salem, Drawer F, Salem Station, 600 Main St.,
Winston-Salem, NC 27108

With its halls decked out as they were 200 years ago, Old Salem returns to the spirit of Christmas past. This national historic landmark, was founded in 1766 by a group of Moravian Germans. Although industrious and religious, they knew how to have a good time, filling their Christmas with carols, food, costumes, laughter and good cheer.

Music is provided by choral and brass ensembles, by bell ringers and a historic 1797 Tanenberg organ. Craft demonstrations, street actors and slide lectures give you a close look at what life was really like in this colonial town—and all the participants wear authentic 18th century costumes. Christmas of old is brought to life, with traditional events like the children's lovefeast and the lighting of pyramids. The Moravian settlement found that Christmas makes everybody just a little hungrier than usual, so they have plenty of authentic goodies for their visitors. The whole family will enjoy this cheerful jaunt into the past.

DECEMBER. 2 weeks

Christmas Island

Jekyll Island, Georgia

Most events free
Contact: Jekyll Island Authority, 375 Riverview Dr.,
Jekyll Island, GA 31520

Travel back in time to Christmas, 1900, when Jekyll Island became Christmas Island. Situated off the coast of southern Georgia, this resort area celebrates a nostalgic holiday. The celebration starts with a tree lighting ceremony and the winking-on of thousands of twinkling lights in the older, historic section of the town. Volunteers from the Garden Club decorate the island with wreaths and garlands of holly, magnolia, cedar, cones and poinsettias. Jekyll Island Museum

welcomes you to its restored, historic cottages where docents dressed in period attire conduct tours and entertain with Victorian games and dances. Seasonal activities include Christmas decoration workshops, cooking classes, music programs, dances and hayrides. Special theatrical programs are scheduled, including a major stage performance and concert by Jekyll's Big Dance Band. Everyone enjoys singing traditional Christmas songs at the caroling parties. And, of course, you may witness old St. Nicholas' visits to the island.

DECEMBER 1 THROUGH MID-MARCH. Daily

Reelfoot Eagle Tours

Reelfoot Lake State Resort Park, Tennessee

Admission charged
Contact: Director of Information, Tennessee Department of Tourist Development, Room T, Box 23170, Nashville, TN 37202

The majestic Bald Eagle migrates from Canada and the Great lakes to winter at Reelfoot Lake in Tennessee. Its annual return is eagerly anticipated. Attracted by fish hidden in the depths of the lake, the eagles provide the visitor with a rare opportunity to view this awesome species. Reelfoot Lake was formed by a violent earthquake in 1812 when a local valley housing a cypress forest sank 20 feet and was swallowed by backwash from the Mississippi River. The ancient forest is still hidden by the waters and its twisted branches provide a perfect habitat for almost 60 different species of fish. The richness of the lake in turn attracts a wealth of wildlife, especially birds. Eagle tours are conducted seven days a week and special programs with speakers and films introduce the visitor to the biology of the area.

FEBRUARY. 3 days

Eagles Et Cetera

DeGray State Park, Bismarck, Arkansas

Admission charged
Contact: Park Interpreter, DeGray State Park, Rt. 3, Box 490, Bismarck, AR 71929

In the winter, eagles often seek the warmer climes of south-central United States before returning to the far north to breed and raise their young. In February, they can be viewed around the lake at DeGray State Park. These giant predators often reach a wing-span of six to eight feet. Golden Eagles hunt other birds and small mammals, whereas the Bald Eagles live principally on fish. Boat tours and field trips with experienced naturalists offer the visitor a good chance to see these birds of prey as well as other wildlife in the vicinity. Slide shows and talks introduce the basics of bird identification and teach the natural history of specific birds. Many birdwatching specialists are on hand with talks and tips on the sport.

Boating tours are scheduled both Saturday and Sunday, and accomodations are available at the lodge. Make reservations well in advance.

JANUARY THROUGH MARCH. About 2 months

Old Island Days

Key West, Florida

Most events free
Contact: Old Island Restoration Foundation, P.O. Box 689,
Key West, FL 33041

Key West is an old city, southernmost point of continental U.S.A. Surrounded by water, the island's oldtimers call themselves conchs (pronounced 'konks') after the local sea snail. The first fortunes made here were by the wreckers, local seamen who salvaged cargo from ships wrecked on the treacherous reefs. They built homes with a strange mixture of architecture, part New England with a dash of the Bahamas, with lots of porches and rocking chairs. These homes are highlighted during three weekends of Old Islands Days. Old cottages and mansions are opened to the public for tours, along with their exotic tropical gardens.

Another festive occasion during Old Island Days is the boat parade. Elaborately decorated shrimp boats sail out of the harbor to receive a blessing and the community's prayers for a safe year. Following is the Shrimp and Sauce Sampler, with heaping platters of steamed fish and dozens of sauces to choose from. Dessert is not ignored either, your sweet tooth will have a hard time choosing between Key Lime pies, clamondin cake, coconut candy, guava shells with cream cheese or banana pudding. The celebration features other events including an arts expo and a crafts expo, a sidewalk art fair in Old Town, a historical pageant and conch blowing contests.

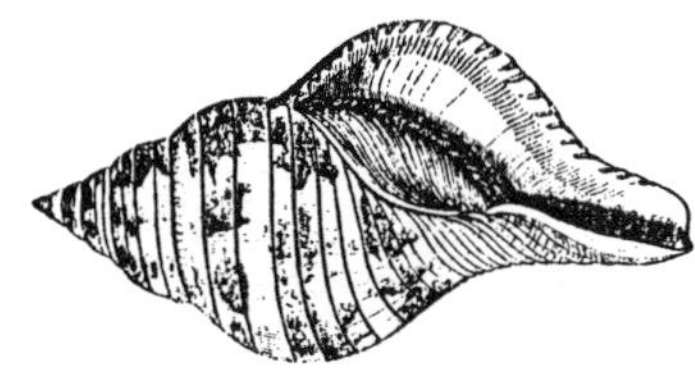

USUALLY FEBRUARY. The two weeks preceeding Ash Wednesday

Mardi Gras

New Orleans, Louisiana

Free
Contact: Greater New Orleans Tourist and Conventions
Commission, 334 Royal Street, New Orleans, LA
70130

Ancient, flamboyant and ritualistic, Mardi Gras is undoubtedly America's most famous carnival. Held the two weeks before Lent, Mardi Gras has been celebrated since the 1700s. Clearly related to European carnivals, Mardi Gras is an enormous street festival. Over 60 private Mardi Gras organizations exist in New Orleans, and most of them stage their own parade and costume ball. The city provides police and sanitation support, but the rest is left to the individual clubs, or 'krewes.' The oldest krewes date from over 100 years ago and follow well-established traditions. Often the membership is secret and the king parades masked. Most krewes have mythological names and new ones continue to appear. Although there is a children's krewe, several for women, and a couple of all-black krewes, the majority of them seem to be all-male.

Parades are public, along certain set routes in New Orleans. Many parades feature special themes that are carefully guarded secrets until the night before. Float and costume designers labor for months in preparation, and all costs are assumed by the krewe. The elaborately costumed members ride floats and toss collectible items to the public, including specially cast doubloons, emblem necklaces and trinkets. The crowds compete to collect the most coins and keepsakes from the largest number of parades.

Traditionally, the costumed balls are private, by invitation only. However, there seems to be a move to open some of the balls to the public by selling tickets. Each ball has a King and Queen who reign over a full court of krewe members. Attire is elaborate and expensive, and most balls continue all night with entertainment and dancing.

Each year the parade floats grow in beauty and complexity. Formerly drawn by mules, they are now pulled by tractors. Night parades are illuminated by *flambeaux*—handheld torchlights. Almost three dozen Walking Clubs are organized to parade on foot during Carnival. Some walk alongside the floats of specific krewes, others march independently, often from bar to bar. Costumed, often accompanied by Dixieland bands, carrying flowers to exchange for kisses, these groups add to the colorful and wild abandon of Mardi Gras.

MARCH. 1 day

Peanut Frolic

Tifton, Georgia

Admission charged
Contact: Georgia Agrirama Development Authority,
P.O. Box Q, Tifton, GA 31793

Here's a way to journey back to the rural South of a hundred years ago. The Georgia Agrirama is a beautifully reconstructed agricultural community of the late 1800's. Antique artifacts and structures have been faithfully restored to duplicate the kind of life our great-grandfathers enjoyed. Open year-round, visitors can explore the barnyard, watch farm life activities from planting to harvesting, view a cotton gin and grist mill, ride a logging train and see skilled craftsmen practise the trades of the times. The Peanut Frolic at Agrirama is a special springtime event celebrating the planting of Georgia's most significant crop. The visitor can enter peanut shelling contests, watch peanut brittle cooking on the wood-burning stove, pop corn around a bonfire or learn the dance steps of the era. Costumed interpreters guide visitors through the village and lead the cotillions and reels of the 1890's. Fiddlers and banjo pickers play old-fashioned tunes from the farmhouse porch as a traditional planting frolic is re-created.

FIRST WEEKEND IN APRIL. 2 days

Blowing Rock Annual Opening Day Trout Derby

Blowing Rock, North Carolina

No entry fee, but valid fishing license required
Contact: Blowing Rock Parks & Recreation, P.O. Box 47,
Blowing Rock NC 28605

Hopeful anglers gather to try their luck on opening day of trout season. In and about Blowing Rock, they cast their lines into the waters, trying to snag the largest trout, or, perhaps, a specially tagged one worth $300. Trophies and merchant prizes are awarded in every division; even little kids can win. On both days, tense participants meet at the Blowing Rock Hardware Store to officially register their catch and check out the competition. Information about public trout waters and the required license can be obtained from the Hardware Store.

EASTER WEEK. 9 days

Easter Festival

St. Augustine, Florida

Free
Contact: Chamber of Commerce, P.O. Drawer O,
St. Augustine, FL 32085

The oldest city in the country, St. Augustine's history stretches back four hundred years to 1565 when the Spanish landed. Much of the city's history is preserved in its architecture and festivals. Palm Sunday begins a week-long celebration observing both historic and religious events. A Royal Trio is selected from St. Augustine's oldest families to represent the city throughout the year and symbolizing Spanish Queen Mariana and her two children.

The festival begins with an arts and crafts sidewalk show exhibiting the works of more than 100 craftsmen. On Palm Sunday, the Bishop officiates at the annual blessing of the fleet at the yacht harbor. Colorfully decorated boats of all descriptions pass in review, followed by a delicious oyster roast. Events continue the week before Easter with frequent performances of a Passion Play and concerts in the bandshell. Saturday brings the annual seafood festival downtown in the historic plaza. Easter is celebrated in a variety of churches, and at a sunrise service atop Castillo de San Marcos. Easter afternoon is climaxed by a unique parade, the *Parado de los Caballos y Coches.* Carriage horses proudly bedecked in splendid Easter bonnets donated by famous women parade along with beautifully decorated floats, stirring bands, drill teams, the sheriff's posse and beauty queens. The next day features a celebration honoring the Minorcan settlers of St. Augustine.

springtime event. Friday and Saturday each have their own popular parade—the first is the biggest Firefighter's Parade in the country, and the second is the elaborate Grand Feature Parade with nearly a hundred bands and dozens of fancifully constructed theme floats. Music is an integral part of the festival, with large competitions for concert bands, field marching bands and jazz ensembles. Celebrities grace the parades and coronation of Queen Shenandoah.

A special Sports Breakfast is held with famous sports personalities in attendance. Evenings bring a variety of dances including the Queen's formal ball, teen dances, a square dance, a country music dance and an informal festival dance with popular music. The festival closes Sunday with events in the park for children. Two stages provide entertainment, an arts and crafts show is set up, an apple crate derby is run, a Civil War battle is re-enacted and food concessions feed the celebrants. In keeping with the theme, tour maps are available for spendid trips through the fragrant orchards of the valley.

APRIL/MAY. 4 days

Shenandoah Apple Blossom Festival

Winchester, Virginia

Admission charged to a few events
Contact: Shenandoah Apple Blossom Festival, P.O. Box 3099,
Winchester, VA 22601

Nothing is more American than an Apple Blossom Festival, and Virginia celebrates with a stupendous

tour information and educational exhibits. Educational kits highlighting the history and culture of the country are prepared and circulated to local schools. Often performing artists and dance troupes will visit Birmingham, and local arts groups feature the traditions and forms of the honored country in their performances. A gala dinner honoring the U.S. ambassador from the guest country opens this artistic and cultural exchange.

APRIL/MAY. 10 days

New Orleans Jazz & Heritage Festival

New Orleans, Louisiana

Admission charged to evening concerts and Heritage Fair
Contact: New Orleans Jazz & Heritage Festival, Box 2530,
1205 North Rampart St., New Orleans LA 70176

The air of New Orleans reverberates with the same kind of excitement that spawned jazz, dixieland, rhythm'n blues and gospel so many years ago. This

huge music festival draws 3,000 musicians, local artists as well as scores of well-known names from around the world. Evening concerts are held in various jazz clubs, theatres and aboard the Riverboat President. Ray Charles, Pete Fountain, Gato Barbieri, Etta James, Herbie Mann and Woody Shaw have all been recent headliners. On both weekends, Heritage Fair is held on the park-like infield of the Fair Grounds Race Track. Here nine stages of simultaneous music play at all times featuring such names as Bo

APRIL/MAY. 10 days

Birmingham Festival of Arts

Birmingham, Alabama

Admission charged to some events
Contact: Festival of Arts, Commerce Center, 9th Floor, 2027
1st Avenue North, Birmingham, AL 35203

One of the America's oldest art festivals, the Birmingham festival, each year honors the culture and art of a different nation. Past honorees have included Mexico, Canada, most of the European countries, Japan, India, Nigeria and Israel. With a truly international flavor, the Birmingham festival each year organizes specific events to showcase the art of the honored country. The Birmingham Museum of Art mounts a major display of the art of the country and other exhibits are shown around town. The Alabama Symphony Orchestra plays a special concert, often with guest artists from the featured country. An International Fair is held with arts and crafts shows, ethnic food, special activities,

Diddley, Fats Domino, Rita Coolidge and Jerry Lee Lewis. Mouthwatering Louisiana specialty foods are sold at the fair, and hundreds of folk artists sell and demonstrate their crafts.

FIRST SUNDAY IN MAY. 1 day

Ramp Festival

Cosby, Tennessee

Admission charged
Contact: Dr. Jack A. Clark, 320 E. Broadway, Newport, TN 37821

The wild ramp is the first spring vegetable to appear in the hills of east Tennessee. A native onion with lance-shaped leaves and a root bulb, ramp is sweet to eat, somewhat a cross between onion, leek and garlic. However, it has a powerful and pungent odor which has won it an equally powerful reputation. Mountain dwellers of the region believe it will prevent the common cold while critics claim ramp-eaters smell so bad they can't get close enough to anyone else to catch a cold. Whatever its therapeutic value, wild ramp is celebrated in this spring festival in the Great Smokey Mountains. Country foods are cooked, barbecued chicken, corn pone and, of course, the ramp. Music includes gospel, country, bluegrass and rock'n roll. A prince and princess are crowned, along with a little Maid of Ramps. The celebration has attracted

political personalities, including several governors, and entertainment celebrities. Run by a non-profit club, all proceeds are used to help the area's needy.

SECOND WEEKEND IN MAY. 3 days

The International Strange Music Weekend

Carter Caves State Park, Kentucky

Admission charged to concert, contest free
Contact: Carter Caves State Park, Olive Hill, KY 41164

Nothing is beneath a strange musician; not playing corn cans, pop bottles, snoot flutes or even pennywhistles inside a gas mask. Carter Caves State Park boasts many natural wonders (beautiful wildflowers, babbling brooks, sport fishing in a glorious lake, and the awesome subterranean caves), but it is more famous for the unnatural wonders of strange music. Each year the amphitheatre seats more people as word gets around, the concert has even been featured on CBS News. The next day a contest with real prizes is held for the most clever homemade musical instrument. This weekend is perfect for folk who like songs about pond scum or who positively delight in a tune played on toy chainsaws. You may even want to bring a washtub or a kazoo and join the fun.

Memphis in May

Memphis, Tennessee

Free
*Contact: Memphis in May, 245 Wagner Pl., Suite 220,
Memphis, TN 38103*

Canada, Germany, Venezuela, Egypt, The Netherlands, Israel, Mexico, Australia and Japan! The Old South takes on a definite international flavor each year as Memphis in May honors a foreign nation. The culture of Memphis and the guest country are showcased side by side in a month of exciting weekend events. This enormous celebration (1985 saw a million visitors) takes place in parks, squares and malls all over Memphis, including an island in the middle of the Mississippi River. One weekend highlights the visiting culture as a park is transformed into a mini-replica of the country, complete with its unique cuisine, crafts, goods and performers. Athletes delight in a day of amateur athletic events, including an official 10k run, fun runs, relays and the 'world's largest aerobics class.' A triathlon is held another weekend. One weekend is reserved for children of all ages with art, music and educational events on Mud Island.

The middle of the month brings the most hotly contested barbecue cookoff in the world. Contestants compete for cash prizes for the best grilled hog, shoulder or ribs. Hog callers also gather, and Ms. Piggie is crowned queen. Memphis' musical heritage is proudly displayed during the Beale Street Music Festival with concerts ranging from blues to rock to gospel. Memphis in May concludes with a concert in the park by the Memphis Symphony Orchestra saluting the music and citizens of the honored country.

Shrimp Festival

Fernandina Beach, Florida

Admission charged to some events
*Contact: Chamber of Commerce, P.O. Box 472, Fernandina
Beach, FL 32034*

Fernandina Beach on Amelia Island contains only a few thousand souls, yet it hosts the major festival in northern Florida. Over 100,000 people travel here in May for the Shrimp Festival. Tons and tons of delicious seafood are consumed, both in the area's restaurants and in the many food booths downtown. The first evening opens with a dramatic invasion of costumed pirates commemorating some of the less-civilized among the island's early tourists. This is followed by a giant fireworks display over the river.

The Shrimp Ball is also held that night. An art and antique craft show runs the weekend, and various concerts and theatrical performances are presented. The adventuresome festival-goer can ride in a helicopter, a boat on the Amelia River, and in the gondola of a hot air balloon. A fun run and a beach run are also held. Both beauties and beards have their own separate contests. A festive boat parade travels down the river, and the fishing fleet is blessed on Sunday. Nearby Fort Clinch State Park offers free admission during the celebration.

MAY. 10 days

Woodchopping Festival

Webster Springs, West Virginia

Free

Contact: Woodchopping Festival, P.O. Box 227, Webster Springs, WV 26288

Balancing on planks high above the ground, brawny woodsmen try to chop through tree trunks in record time as part of the World Championship Woodchopping Contest. Entrants from around the world travel to this festival to win points in such categories as hot saw, two-man crosscut, underhand standing block and the spring board. These displays of chippin' and choppin' are not all the festival, however. Miss Woodchopper and Little Miss Woodchip pageants are held, and firemen parade down the street followed by a state championship fireman's rodeo. The visitor can consume a lumberjack breakfast and attend an arts and crafts show. Musical events include square dancing, gospel singing and a crooner's cabaret. To top it off, the state championship Turkey Calling Contest is held in the county courtroom.

☀ SUMMER ☀

JUNE. 1 week

Billy Bowlegs Festival

Fort Walton Beach, Florida

Free

Contact: Chamber of Commerce, 34 Miracle Strip Parkway, S.E., Fort Walton Beach, FL 32548

Pirates and plundering Indians still rampage the Florida coast. A flotilla with hundreds of costumed pirates lands on the beach each June in re-creation of the arrival of Captain Billy Bowlegs (William Bowles) over two hundred years ago. Captain Bowlegs fought the English, Spanish and French for claim to the territory. He set up his own throne and robbed the ships of any nation who dared to come near. His reign is riotously re-enacted each year starting with the boat parade and 'sacking' of the city.

A festive torchlight parade is held, as well as a children's parade. You can stroll through an international food fair and a pirate's market. Competitors can enter a raft race, sailboat regatta, fishing rodeo, tennis tournament, swim meet, golf tournament or various runs. Captain Billy and his Queen are crowned, as is little Miss Pirate. In a very popular event, treasure maps are sold and eager hunters search the area all week for hidden prizes. Captain Billy died without revealing the location of his booty, perhaps some year it will be uncovered amongst the festival prizes.

JULY. 1 day

Hillbilly Day

Mountain Rest, South Carolina

Free
Contact: Mountain Rest Community Club, Mountain Rest, SC
29664

Hillbillies are an endangered species, except in South Carolina where they have their own festival. Hillbilly hospitality is as lively as their music, so plenty of other folks make their way to Mountain Rest, too. The fun includes such countrified events as an egg toss, a shoe kick, races and a tug-of-war, the greased pole climb and the greased pig chase. Traditional music is played and old-time costumes are worn. Clog dancers stomp to the tunes of a bluegrass group. Souvenirs are sold at the country store alongside a pioneer display. Traditional crafts are shown, with drawings for a handmade quilt and a Remington shotgun. Hungry visitors can purchase barbecued chicken, or Brunswick stew before making their way to the cake shack. Demonstrations include blacksmithing, basket making, quilting and soap making. An operating still shows how corn liquor was made in the good old days, and a grist mill grinds flour and meal.

LAST WEDNESDAY AND THURSDAY IN JULY. 2 days

Chincoteague Annual Carnival & Pony Penning

Chincoteague Island, Virginia

Free
Contact: Public Relations Chairman, Box 558 East Side,
Chincoteague, Virginia, 23336

Decades ago, two disastrous fires almost destroyed the town of Chincoteague. Concerned citizens created a Volunteer Fire Company and hit upon a carnival and pony auction to support their services. The carnival occurs nightly during the last two weeks of July, and features all the usual rides and games as well as such local specialties as oyster sandwiches. Then, on the last Wednesday in July, members of the fire department round up the wild ponies living on a nearby island and herd them into the water. The ponies swim across the channel to Chincoteague where the first to arrive is crowned King or Queen Neptune. The next day, a pony auction is held followed by the wild pony rides. After these events, the remaining wild horses are swum back to their island to await next year's carnival.

AUGUST. 3 days

Appalachian Arts & Crafts Festival

Beckley, West Virginia

Contact: County Chamber of Commerce, P.O. Box 1798, Beckley, WV 25802

Arts and crafts are thriving in Appalachia. Such pursuits as pine needle baskets, decorated egg shells, chainsaw sculpture, cornhusk dolls, painted china, silk flower miniatures and scrimshaw jewelry are kept alive by devoted craftsmen. Beautifully designed and patiently crafted quilts are shown, and some handmade quilted goods are for sale. Traditional Appalachian foods and live entertainment are also featured. In the nearby area the visitor can see a performance at the outdoor theatre and tour historic coal mine exhibits.

Strange Seafood Exhibition

North Carolina Maritime Museum

Beaufort, North Carolina

Admission charged. Only 1,000 tickets sold, advance tickets go on sale in May
Contact: North Carolina Maritime Museum, 120 Turner Street, Beaufort, NC 28516

What is 'strange' seafood? According to the North Carolina Maritime Museum it includes traditional foods no longer eaten, seafoods known only to local old-timers, foods harvested in North Carolina but exported to gourmets in other countries, plus new or unusual preparations of old favorites. Specifically, the visitor to this exhibition can sample such strange dishes as sea lettuce soup, pinfish tidbits, raw sea urchins, stingray casserole or shark salad. To help ease the confusion in your kitchen, demonstrations are held on the cleaning and preparation of crucial ingredients. The visitor can buy a cookbook with recipes, illustrations of how and where to catch the ingredients and cooking instructions. All seafoods are gathered from the North Carolina coast and seem strange only until they have been sampled.

Raw purple sea urchins being served at the Strange Seafood Exhibition.

Louisiana Shrimp & Petroleum Festival

Morgan City, Louisiana

Free
Contact: Louisiana Shrimp and Petroleum Festival, P.O. Box 103, Morgan City, LA 70381

The waters of the Gulf provide a livelihood for many residents of the port town of Morgan City. Shrimp trawlers have been making a living here since the discovery of jumbo shrimp in the area in 1933, and the first successful oil well was drilled offshore in 1947. The annual Shrimp and Petroleum Festival celebrates these two industries and their impact on the area.

Heart of the celebration is the blessing of the fleet and water parade. Gaily decorated fishing boats and oil industry craft parade on Berwich Bay to receive the Bishop's blessing. The city hosts many other events, including a street fair with rides, games, food booths, entertainment and free street dances. A photo contest and artists' show are held. Many events are designed to delight children, including a morning of field sports and games, storytime in the bandstand and a children's mini-parade with kid-sized floats designed and decorated by local neighborhoods. If you're energetic you can attend a square dance or the coronation ball, and the next day run a 5k race. A gala street parade marches up Second Street with bands, floats and queens. The festival ends with a spectacular fireworks show.

SEPTEMBER. 2 days

Festivals Acadians

Lafayette, Louisiana

Admission charged
Contact: Convention and Visitors Commission, P.O. Box 52066, Lafayette, LA 70505

The Acadians were French-Canadians who emigrated from Nova Scotia to Louisiana when Canada became British. Arriving in the South, their culture intermixed with that of the Spanish, Indian and African people of the region, resulting in that unique blend known as Cajun. Lafayette's celebration is really seven mini-fests combined into one large tribute to its Cajun heritage. The heart of the festival is the Cajun Music Festival with some of America's hottest Cajun and *zydeco* musicians performing. Young musicians from all over the country travel here to learn more about this traditional music and its mixed roots.

The Bayou Food Festival features native cuisine cooked by dozens of local restaurateurs, chefs and caterers. Visitors can sample crawfish *etouffe*, blackened red fish, crawfish soup, seafood gumbo, crab claws and frog legs. The University Art Museum sponsors the Deep South Writer's Conference where original works of poetry and fiction are read. The

Museum also presents a one-act play and several performances of a local dance company. Lafayette's Natural History Museum hosts a native crafts festival. Here artisans demonstrate crafts from the 19th century such as pirogue making, blacksmithing, weaving and spinning, soap making, quilting and fiddle making. Modern and antique Cajun musical instruments will also be displayed.

The Acadian Village is a Cajun folk museum and presents special activities throughout the festival, including many geared toward children. A Senior Citizen's Fair and Craft Show is also held, and the Jaycees sponsor an annual trade show displaying various local businesses and industries. In keeping with the Cajun theme, the trade show is opened by dignitaries ceremonially cutting a 25-foot *boudin*, a spicy local sausage. You will also find pony rides, a midway and a petting zoo. Saluted as one of America's Top 100 festivals in 1984, over 75,000 people annually attend Festivals Acadians.

Frank Smith, 117-year-old storyteller.

THIRD WEEKEND IN SEPTEMBER. 2 days

Corn Island Storytelling Festival

Louisville, Kentucky

Admission charged
Contact: Corn Island Storytelling Festival, 133 Outer Loop, Louisville, KT 40214.

Like a fantasy come true, you can steam down the Ohio River on a paddle-wheeler with a fabled collection of yarnspinners and tellers of tall tales. The first event of this festival cruises down the river as the storytellers warm up to their art. Located at several different historic spots in Louisville, this festival brings practicioners of the ancient art from all over the country. On Saturday all the storytellers perform at the Locust Grove. Also at this site is a special children's corner where you can hear new storytellers just learning the art as well as centenarians who have been spinning yarns all their long lives.

Speaking of yarns, there is even a Yarn Shop where amateurs can practise their skills. The visitor can also find an arts and crafts display, a delicious auction of old-fashioned pies and barbecue foods for purchase. The concluding event, guaranteed to run a shiver up your spine, is a hair-raising telling of ghost stories amidst the tombstones at the Long Run Cemetery after the sun has gone down.

Queen Sugar XLII, Theresa Gascon.

LATE SEPTEMBER. 3 days

Louisiana Sugar Cane Festival

New Iberia, Louisiana

Free
Contact: Louisiana Sugar Cane Festival, P.O. Box 675, New Iberia, LA 70560

Bringing in the harvest is sweet work in New Iberia as the sugar canes are cut and trucked in from local farms. The last weekend in September brings the Sugar Cane Festival, probably the sweetest festival in the country. A Sugar Queen and King Sucrose are crowned, while various Sugar Lumps are selected to represent the community. A Farmer's Day is held with the blessing of the cane crop, an agricultural homemaking show and a contest among the farmers for the highest yield. The festival holds four parades —a boat parade on the bayou, an agricultural parade, a Queen's parade and the joyous children's parade. Events conclude the final night with a big fireworks display.

National Storytelling Festival

Jonesborough, Tennessee

Admission charged
Contact: National Storytelling Resource Center, P.O. Box 112, Slemons House, Fox Street, Jonesborough, TN 37659

The oldest town west of the Alleghenies is the site of this festival celebrating the ancient art of storytelling. Developed to a high degree in Appalachia in past centuries, live storytelling survives despite modern addiction to TV. In brightly striped tents, performers take to the stage to bring the wonders of their tales alive. The audience is caught up in the atmosphere of the story, sees the essential truths behind the fanciful exaggerations, and laughs with delight at the trick endings. Two-century-old Jonesborough is the perfect antique setting for the festival, and visitors can stroll down Main Street between concerts. A dozen or so professional yarn-spinners headline the festival each year. Amateur storytellers can visit the Swappin' Ground and share their stories anytime on Saturday. Spine-tingling ghost stories are uttered at the old Jonesborough cemetery on Saturday night. Sunday afternoon concludes with storytelling in the park.

Dozens of master storytellers from all over spin their tales at the National Storytelling Festival.

OCTOBER. 3 days

Gumbo Festival

Bridge City, Louisiana

Admission, parking and entertainment are free
Contact: Gumbo Festival, 328 Wiegand Dr., Westwego, LA 70094

Gumbo is the quintessential example of native Cajun cooking, an amalgam of cultural influences that ends up being greater than the sum of its parts. The name derives from an African word for ocra, the ingredients are French, Spanish and Indian with room left over for individual improvisations. Bridge City cooks its gumbo in a 400-gallon pot, enough to feed the tens of thousands who annually flock to the Gumbo Festival. Two thousand gallons of seafood and chicken gumbo are the stars of the festival, however, Cajuns love food and there are plenty of other local specialties, too. Try the secret-recipe potato salad, jambalaya, red beans and rice, oyster loaves or buttered corn on the cob. Local cooks compete in gumbo, pie and cake contests. A carnival is held and the stage offers continuous live entertainment all three days. A beautiful child contest is held each day, and Queen Creole Gumbo is on hand to greet festival-goers.

OCTOBER. 2 days

Tennessee Valley Old-Time Fiddlers Convention

Athens, Alabama

Admission charged
Contact: TVOTFC, Athens State College, Athens, AL 35611

Old time music is still cherished at the Fiddlers Convention. Ignoring the last couple of centuries or so, contestants keep alive the traditional songs and forms. Competing for their share of a $7,000 purse, hundreds of fiddlers, banjo players, buck dancers, harmonica blowers, mandolin pickers, singers and band members gather at Athens State College. Informal jam sessions and concerts develop during the two days as musicians wait their turn on the stage. A traditional arts and crafts festival awaits you with an Appalachian herbalist displaying mountain lore.

War Eagle Fair

Hindsville, Arkansas

Free
Contact: Ozark Arts and Crafts Fair Association, War Eagle
Mills Farm, Rt. 1, Hindsville, AK 72738

Across the old arched iron bridge, next to the white barn, are the brilliantly colored striped tents of the War Eagle Fair. Nestled in the hills of the Ozarks, the fair started some 30 years ago as an amateur weaving exhibit. It now presents the crafts of some 500 artisans, but still retains the friendly, down-home atmosphere of the first years. Open to artists from a four-state area—Arkansas, Missouri, Oklahoma and Kansas—War Eagle is devoted to preserving the indigenous crafts of the area. Some exhibitors have attended every fair for 30 years. From afghans to wreaths, applique to woodworking, most American

Various stringed instruments, hand-built by L.O. Stapleton.

handcrafts are represented here, and each artist is carefully juried to ensure quality of work. You'll find no manufactured hobby kits or plastic at War Eagle. Even the Smithsonian has visited War Eagle to view the crafts. The three-day event takes place when the rolling hills of the Ozarks are at their most brilliant.

Perryville Battlefield Celebration & Re-Enactment

Perryville, Kentucky

Free
Contact: Perryville Battlefield State Shrine, Perryville
KY 40468

Each year the Blue and Gray once again don their uniforms, polish their muskets and face each other in this re-enactment of a bloody Civil War battle. In 1862, Kentucky saw its most desperate military event as the Confederates marched into the state. Union forces defeated them in Perryville, and the visitor can watch these batallions clash again. This battlefield celebration also features various military drill, uniform and camp competitions. For the ladies there is a tea and dress display. In the nearby town of Perryville, you can see the historic merchants section. The actual battlefields are located in a state park with ample picnic facilities, hiking trails, a Civil War museum and gift shop.

Fall Chrysanthemum Extravaganza

Bellingrath Gardens, Theodore, Alabama

Admission charged
Contact: Bellingrath Gardens and Home, Route 1, Box 60,
Theodore, AL 36582

A gracious southern estate, Bellingrath annually displays its hospitality with thousands of chrysanthemums in full bloom. Each November the old brick mansion and 60 acres of landscaped gardens blossom forth with the greatest outdoor display of flowers in the South. Manicured paths and walkways are edged with blooms and dramatic cascades spill over the balconies of the old brick mansion. Inside, you can browse through collections of antiques, fine china and the world's largest collection of Boehm porcelain.

Mid-West

International Peace Garden
Minot
NORTH DAKOTA
Bismarck
Fargo
Duluth
MINNESOTA
Sauk Centre
St. Cloud
Minneapolis
St. Paul
Shakopee
WISCONSIN
Green Bay
SOUTH DAKOTA
Pierre
Rapid City
Worthington
Sioux Falls
Fond du Lac
Cedarburg
Milwaukee
Madison
Monroe
MICHIGAN
Grand Rapids
Lansing
Detroit
Kalamazoo
Britt
Decorah
IOWA
Cedar Rapids
Freeport
Oregon
Chicago
Cleveland
Nappanee
Des Moines
NEBRASKA
Omaha
Madison County
Valparaiso
Fort Wayne
Mansfield
Coshocton
OHIO
Kewanee
Lafayette
Van Buren
Columbus
Circleville
Nelsonville
Lincoln
ILLINOIS
Noblesville
Cincinnati
Springfield
INDIANA
Rio Grande
Hannibal
Arcola
Bloomington
Canaan
Kansas City
Independence
Topeka
St. Louis
KANSAS
MISSOURI
Wichita
Springfield

Street festivities at the Circleville Pumpkin Show.

Bucksaw contest in Canaan, Indiana.

Minneapolis Aquatennial's Milk Carton Boat Race.

Eagle Creek Rendezvous.

Grandstand show at Festa Italiana.

JANUARY. 1 week

Winter Festival

Omaha, Nebraska

Most events free
Contact: Parks, Recreation & Public Property Department,
1819 Farnam St., Omaha, NE 68183

With the ringing slogan of 'Participate, Don't Hibernate,' Omaha's major winter festival encourages people to get outside and enjoy the weather. As a matter of fact, bad weather for this celebration and its many outdoor events would be warm weather. Fresh snow with clear, chilly days are ideal here. Most activities take place on Cunningham Lake. The festival starts with a parade to the lake and the crowning of the Snow Queen. Motorized, winter-adapted events draw thousands of spectators to watch motorcycle races, funny car races, hang gliding, radio controlled airplanes and ultralights. Ice skating

competitions and exhibitions, ice hockey games, figure skating competitions, ice fishing contests, speed skating races, ice canoe races, cross country skiing, ice fishing, toboganing, sledding and snowshoeing all beckon the visitor. Eager competitors even demonstrate the gentle art of 'snurfing'—skateboarding on the snow. The public is further lured outside by outdoor survival training, horse-drawn sleigh rides and dog sled rides. Most everybody wants cold weather for festival week.

JANUARY. 2 days

Lakeside Winter Celebration

Fond du Lac, Wisconsin

Free
Contact: Convention & Visitors Bureau, 207 N. Main St.,
Fond du Lac, WI 54935

Lake Winnebago freezes solid each winter, and celebrants take to its icy surface for many of these events. Ice bowling, broom ball, three- and four-wheeler races and motorcycle ice races are held on the lake. Visitors can also watch snowmobile races or ride in horse-drawn carriages. Sled dogs compete to pull the most weight. All the outdoor activities awaken large appetites, and the park is full of hot food concessions and a chili cook-off to stave off hunger pangs.

a torch parade down the slopes. The next day men have a chance to display their bravado in the Super Skier Tri-Slam. The event starts with an uphill climb on skis while carrying a weighted pack, followed by a downhill slalom. This winner is the first to raise his glass of beer upon reaching the bottom of the course. The Ohio Ski Queen is crowned this weekend. However, the entire weekend isn't given over to zaniness. Regular skiing continues and the ski school gives demonstrations both days.

FEBRUARY. 2 days

Winter Ski Carnival

Mansfield, Ohio

Admission charged
Contact: Snow Trails Ski Resort, Box 163, Mansfield, OH
44901

When snowbound midwesterns grow weary of huddling around the fireplace and dreaming of tropic isles, they take to the slopes for a weekend of outdoor festivities. This is the state's largest winter festival, held at Ohio's oldest ski resort. The most popular event, at least from the spectator's viewpoint, is the Bikini Race. All entrants receive a bottle of sun tan lotion and the winner is awarded a new ski outfit. Viewers also enjoy the Mogul Challenge where free-style skiers perform their acrobatics on mogul-filled slopes. The same evening brings a dance followed by

❄ *SPRING* ❄

MARCH. 1 week

Kalamazoo Bach Festival

Kalamazoo, Michigan

Admission charged
Contact: Bach Festival Society, 1200 Academy St., Kalamazoo,
MI 49007

Each year Kalamazoo presents a varied program of baroque music, concentrating on Bach masterpieces and featuring both local performers and guest artists. The first concert is a showcase for the winners of the Young Artists Competition. Invitations are mailed in the fall and auditions take place in January. Each year brings a chamber music concert, often a chorale concert and a Saturday concert of a major Bach work with an intermission dinner. The Kalamazoo Festival is the work of one of the oldest Bach societies in the country and has been presenting the work of this 18th century genius for 25 successive years.

MID-APRIL TO MID-SEPTEMBER. Every weekend.

Ethnic Festivals

Detroit, Michigan

Free
Contact: City of Detroit, Department of Public Information,
608 City-County Building, Detroit, MI 48226

The whole world comes to Hart Plaza in Detroit. Located on the Detroit River, one of the busiest inland waterways in the world, Hart Plaza hosts ethnic festivals every weekend all summer. Gaily decorated booths on the lower level sell food and drinks. The amphitheatre and two stages showcase musicians, dancers, singers and theatrical productions, all representative of the ethnic group displaying that weekend. Representatives from Polish, German, Afro-American, Italian, Slovak, Japanese, Korean, Irish, Greek, Mexican, Indian, Armenian, Far Eastern, Arab and Latin American groups have all participated. The visitor can also enjoy a display booth highlighting the heritage of each group where crafts, costumes and history are displayed.

MAY. 1 day

International Chicken Flying Meet

Rio Grande, Ohio

Free
Contact: Int'l. Chicken Flying Assoc., 3776 S. High St.,
Columbus, OH 43207

Most folks fly kites in spring, but some eggceptional characters fly chickens on Bob Evans' Ohio farm. Speggtators were awe-struck in 1979 when one entrant flew over 302 feet. This record has stood since, despite the lure of a $500 prize. Twenty-three states have official chicken flying squadrons, but this is the eggciting Olympics of the sport. The day starts off with rooster and human crowing contests. Later, chickens compete in a 40-yard jog, and then the main event! Birds are launched from mailboxes with no more persuasion than that offered by a plumber's helper. After the flight, the distance is measured and officially recorded by the ICFA. Birds are classed according to weight, and no eggsperience is required to join this annual eggstravaganza.

Ricky Smith, storyteller.

MAY. 4 days

St. Louis Storytelling Festival

St. Louis, Missouri

Free
Contact: University of Missouri-St. Louis Public Information,
8001 Natural Bridge Rd., St. Louis, MO 63121

"People like to listen," says the originator of the St. Louis Storytelling Festival. And listen they do, with rapt attention, as professional storytellers weave their tales. Located in the famous Gateway Arch at the entrance to the city, this festival opens magical windows into other cultures and lives through the wonderful art of storytelling. Ghosts come haunting, the devil tempts the unwary, loves are won and lost, the wily coyote again stalks the land and river nymphs flirt with mortals. The stories are a living link with our past and charm listeners with their originality and power, especially in this electronic age of predigested entertainment.

LATE MAY. 3 days

Eagle Creek Rendezvous

Shakopee, Minnesota

Admission charged.
Contact: Murphy's Landing, Box 275, Shakopee, MN 55379

Over 150 years ago, fur trades and Indians were the main inhabitants of this area of Minnesota. Today, their lives are authentically re-enacted each year at Murphy's Landing. The visitor can view over 40 large tepees, learn how to shoot a musket, start a fire with flint and steel or barter for handmade trade goods along the banks of the Minnesota River. Restored structures from the mid-1800s will be staffed with tour guides, and the visitor can stroll through an authentic working trading post of that era.

JUNE. 1 day

A Taste of Bloomington

Bloomington, Indiana

Admission charged, and food coupons sold
Contact: Bloomington/Monroe County Convention & Visitors Bureau, 441 Gourley Pike, Bloomington, IN 47401

Mouth-watering treats are dispensed all afternoon and into the evening at Bloomington's annual Taste. Hungry visitors can sample from the offerings of 40 different restaurants. Local wineries, beer and soft drink distributors are on hand to quench your thirst. Pizza slices, fruit crepes, homemade ice cream, barbecue chicken and ribs, fudge, shish kabob, grouper, gyros, hamburgers, fresh pasta, tacos and old fashioned cookies are some of the menu items. Bands, clowns, strolling musicians and a magician entertain contin-

uously. In the middle of the afternoon, Waiter/ Waitress races are held with restaurants competing fiercely for first prize. And, an art fair is featured at the Courthouse Square.

JUNE AND JULY. Friday evenings.

International Festival of the Arts

International Peace Garden, North Dakota and Manitoba, Canada

Admission charged
Contact: International Music Camp, Box 27, Bottineau, ND 58318

Near the geographical center of North America, on the border between United States and Canada, the International Peace Garden is a moving symbol of the harmony between the two nations. This large park with formal gardens, natural landscapes and two lakes also houses a chapel and several theatres. Each summer the International Music Camp conducts classes at the Peace Garden and holds a weekly Festival of the Arts. The festival opens with an old time fiddler's contest, drawing contestants from all areas of both countries. Other events include an amateur art exhibit, ballet performances, choral and symphonic concerts, big band performances and an old-fashioned ice cream social. Picnicking, camping and hiking facilities, food concessions and souvenir shops are available.

JUNE/JULY. 2 weeks

International Freedom Festival

Detroit, Michigan and Windsor, Ontario

Free
Contact: International Freedom Festival, 100 Renaissance Center, Suite 1760, Detroit, MI 48243

Separated only by the river, the two cities of Detroit and Windsor annually celebrate the two great national holidays of their respective countries—Canada Day on July 1st and Independence Day on July 4th.

Designed to promote their mutual heritage of freedom, this border-spanning festival is celebrated by millions of people each year. An International Village is set up with food, crafts and ethnic entertainment from over 30 countries. A replica of an 18th century trapper's village resides in Windsor, complete with Indians and mountain men. One day is dedicated entirely to children with special events, shows, games storytelling and demonstrations. The festival also includes athletic events, tugboat races on the river, parades, an air show, concerts and much more. Capping the entire two weeks is a huge fireworks show, the largest in North America, with colorful pyrotechnics bursting jubilantly over the river.

Independence Day

Conner Prairie Settlement, Noblesville, Indiana

Admission charged
Contact: Conner Prairie Pioneer Settlement, 30 Conner Lane,
Noblesville, IN 46060

It is hard to imagine, late in the 20th century, what pioneer life on the great prairies was like 150 years ago. Fortunately, the curious can visit the Conner Prairie Settlement to view an authentic re-creation of a historic village, complete with costumed residents. A festive Independence Day celebration is staged each year. Village residents perform their interpretations of the meaning of the holiday. The Declaration of Independence is read and a patriotic parade of riflemen, drums and fifes marches along the winding streets. In the evening, the Indianapolis Symphony Orchestra performs and a large fireworks display is set off over the prairie.

OVERLAPPING JULY 4TH. 5 days

Tom Sawyer Days

Hannibal, Missouri

Free
Contact: Hannibal Tourism Commission, P.O. Box 624,
Hannibal MO 63401

People of all ages come to Tom Sawyer Days to act like kids again. Located in Mark Twain's home town,

most of the major events are geared to children as the festival becomes a celebration of America's youth. Events are drawn from Twain's famous novel and include a national fence-painting contest, a Tom and Becky raft race on the Mississippi, and the Hannibal frog jump-off. Visitors can also watch an Old Fiddlers Contest, attend an ice cream social or play mud volleyball. The festival climaxes the fourth of July with a grand parade and, in the evening, a rousing fireworks display.

JULY. 3 days

Nordic Fest

Decorah, Iowa

Admission charged to some events
Contact: Nordic Fest, Inc., P.O. Box 364, Decorah, IA 52101

Uff da is a useful bit of Norwegian meaning 'good grief' and you will find it plastered all over T-shirts and other memorabilia during Nordic Fest. Over a hundred years ago, Norwegian immigrants settled in the picturesque hills of northeast Iowa bringing their arts and crafts, traditions and legends with them. Each year this heritage is celebrated in a festive weekend of activities. Folk artists and performers from Norway come to participate, and the local inhabitants work hard to keep the old ways alive. A big parade is followed by a *lutefisk*-eating contest and all politicians riding in the parade have to promise to stay on later for the (slimy) *lutefisk*. The weekend calendar is filled with cooking and craft demonstra-

tions. Puppet shows, plays, Nordic dancing and choral sings will delight everyone. Most churches in the area stage elaborate smorgasbord feasts with all the home-made food you can eat at reasonable costs.

Nordic Fest is the site of the only Troll Walks in the United States. These walks are conducted daily, and visitors receive a card with a 'Trollfree' number to use in any future troll sightings. *Uff da!*

of the strangest craft to ever take to the water (would you believe a VW on pontoons?).

Landlubbers will find plenty to entertain them, too, with art fairs, concerts, dance demonstrations, a 10k run, games and fun in the park, roller skating events, waitress/waiter races, a bicycle tour and comedy performances. Throughout the festival, daily clues are broadcast hinting at the location of a carefully hidden medallion worth $500. Saturday morning sees a joyous parade with enough bands, floats and crazy rafts to delight everyone.

JULY. 4 days

Wheels, Wings & Water Festival

St. Cloud, Minnesota

Most events free
Contact: Chamber of Commerce, Box 487, St. Cloud, MN
56302

No mere earthbound celebration, the St. Cloud festival also takes to the skies and wends its way over wavelets of the Mississippi River. Participants with their heads in the clouds can ride a hot air balloon or an airplane, and then come back to earth over pancakes and sausage at the airport. Fans of water sports can enter a canoe race, fish for a specially marked fish worth $10,000, witness an AAU swim meet, view an elaborate water ski show with demonstrations and many a fancy trick, enjoy a sailing regatta or watch the KCLD River Raft Race with some

JULY. 4 days

Festa Italiana

Milwaukee, Wisconsin

Admission charged
Contact: Italian Community Center, 2648 North Hackett,
Milwaukee WI 53211

No one leaves Festa Italiana hungry! Almost 30 food

booths sell such mouthwatering specialties as pizza, fried calamari, lasagne, fresh pasta, minestrone, ravioli and spumoni. This giant festival originated in a spirit of community pride after redevelopment and freeway construction had leveled much of the traditional Italian neighborhood in Milwaukee. The biggest Italian festival in the country, and the first of Milwaukee's successful ethnic festivals, Festa brings this large ethnic population back together to celebrate its heritage. Located at the Milwaukee Lakefront, it is four days of feasting and entertainment.

The Lakefront's eight stages feature entertainment from noon to closing each day, making this the largest gathering of Italian performers in the country. They range from local amateur groups to well-known headliners. Choirs and other groups often travel from Rome to perform here. One section of the fairgrounds is for kids only, with a playground and a children's stage showing a balloon clown, Ronald McDonald, a youth talent show and other events. Every night Italian-style fireworks explode in aerial and ground displays, concluding with a spectacular grand finale on Sunday. A solemn high mass is celebrated at noon Sunday, followed by a traditional procession of church organizations carrying shrines and statues. All ticketholders are eligible for the giant raffle.

JULY. 5 days

Sinclair Lewis Days

Sauk Centre, Minnesota

Free
Contact: Chamber of Commerce, P.O. Box 222, Sauk Centre, MN 56378

Time has altered Sauk Centre less than most areas of the country. It has become a living museum of that American institution—the small town. As a boy, America's first Nobel prizewinner for literature, Sinclair Lewis, lived here and permanently memorialized it in his novel *Main Street.* Each July the townspeople celebrate his memory with a festival. A queen is crowned and a parade held, you can visit a flea market or participate in the annual road race. Visitors are encouraged to drop by the Lewis home, furnished in the style of his boyhood, and visit the nearby information center.

MID-JULY. 3 days

Douglas County Historical Steam Festival

Arcola, Illinois

Admission charged
Contact: Fred Nolan, RR # 2, Box 178, Arcola, IL 61910

Watch old-time farming in action, those ancient marvels powered by steam and gas that did the threshing, harvesting and sawmilling. This is History in Motion, showing an array of farm machinery at work on an old Amish Settlement with the 1873 home of Jacob R. Moore at the center. These old iron beasts grunt and groan with exertion as they mow hay, split rails, saw shingles, crush limestone and plow land. They're a wonder to watch as they clank by, exuding billows of hissing steam.

Demonstrations of the 18th and 19th century skills of quilting, chair caning, wool spinning and wheat weaving are almost continuous during this three-day festival. Homemade meals begin at 7 a.m., ample shade is offered along with homemade ice cream and pies. The Peppermill String Band plays country, cajun and bluegrass on Saturday and Sunday, and the Crusaders Quartet performs on Sunday. Children will enjoy the petting zoo, many free rides and searching for potatoes from freshly plowed ground.

The Jacob Moore home was built in the grand style in a Southern tradition with Italianate renaissance influence. It is furnished with mid-Victorian elegance of rosewood, walnut, wild cherry, chestnut and pine. You'll hear puffing engines and a shrill steam whistle long after you leave the Steam Festival.

JULY. 10 days

Minneapolis Aquatennial

Minneapolis, Minnesota

Free
Contact: Minneapolis Aquatennial Association, Commodore Court, 702 Wayzata Blvd., Minneapolis, MN 55403.

With 22 lakes sparkling in the summer sun, Minneapolis is the perfect setting for a giant celebration with 250 free events. Aquatennial annually attracts more than two million visitors. Parade lovers have three big parades to choose from, day or night, land or water. The Grande Day Parade rolls on a Saturday afternoon —a classic parade with queens, bands, clowns and colorful floats. The Torchlight Parade dazzles the spectator on Wednesday night with brightly lit floats. Both have been chosen as among the nations's top-ten parades. The visitor can also settle along the rivershore in the evening to watch the Flotilla Frolic with showboats and other craft decorated with tens of thousands of twinkling lights.

Other aquatic events include water ski shows, a sandcastle contest, sailing and boardsailing regattas and a very popular spectacle where youngsters race in homemade boats constructed from milk cartons.

Landlubbers may want to attend one of the arts fairs, a fashion show, the Queen's coronation, a bike or foot race, one of the many concerts or theatrical performances or a massive block party. Other events include a colorful hot air balloon race drifting over the city, and the fast-paced Formula One Grand Prix powerboat races on the Mississippi River.

Minneapolis Aquatennial Association Sailing Regatta.

LAST WEEKEND IN JULY. 3 days

Old-Time Threshing and Antique Show

Freeport, Illinois

Admission charged
Contact: Stephenson County Antique Engine Club, P.O. Box 83, Freeport, IL 61007

America's agricultural past is re-created here with the display of vintage farming equipment. The festival opens with a parade featuring five men who completely assemble a Model-T Ford in just five minutes. The festival continues for three days and shows you a huge steam-powered sawmill slicing through enormous logs, a stone mill grinding grain and barrel staves being manufactured. Antique tractors and other harvest equipment are displayed, the tractors are featured in the popular tractor pull. Besides steam and gasoline-powered machines, horse-drawn equipment also attracts attention. The exhibit building also holds displays of many specialized antiques, including dolls, toys, household items and clocks. The visitor can also see an old-time machine shop and blacksmithy. The festival re-creates the living history of much of America's farmland.

JULY/AUGUST. 10 days

Ozark Empire Fair

Springfield, Missouri

Admission charged
Contact: Ozark Empire Fair, MPO Box 630, Springfield, MO 65801

In the hot, lazy days of midsummer, crowds flock to Missouri's annual Ozark Empire Fair. Over 200,000 fans attend and entrants come from as far as Texas. One of the nation's premier dairy areas, the cattle shows and judgings remain the heart of the fair.

However, many other interests are also represented. The family living exhibit draws thousands of entrants in such categories as fine arts, photography, hobbies, household arts and floriculture. Whole families gather their photos, children's crafts and favorite fudge recipes for the fair. Street performers — jugglers, clowns, puppet shows, breakdancers — entertain throughout the showgrounds. An air-conditioned performance building houses gospel groups, children's entertainment, fashion shows, traditional Indian dances and marching bands. Free shows daily draw thousands to the grandstand as well.

AUGUST. 3 days

Coshocton Canal Festival

Coshocton, Ohio

Most events free
Contact: Coshocton Canal Festival, PO Box 266, Coshocton, OH 43812

Ride a horse-drawn boat along a restored section of the Ohio Erie Canal. Go back a century or two and visit this unspoiled valley surrounded by wooded hills and imbued with the ageless quality of times when it was inhabited by the Delawares and the Moravians.

The reality of the past has been preserved with horse drawn trolleys in historic brick-paved Roscoe Village lined with old shops. Colorful costumes adorn hundreds of participants and observers throughout the festive weekend. Mid-1800s crafts and activities

are held, along with square dances, old time music, a corn roast, contests, parades, canal boat rides and dozens of other activities. Join the cheering crowds at the several parades and stroll in the most beautiful event of all, the Costume Promenade, a spectacular walk along the tow path of the Ohio Erie Canal in celebration of the opening of the Ohio and Erie Canal over 150 years ago.

AUGUST. 1 day

National Hobo Convention

Britt, Iowa

Free
Contact: Chamber of Commerce, Britt, IA 50423

Mountain Dew, Hobo Bill, Steamtrain Maury, Sparky Smith. The Hardrock Kid, The Philadelphia Kid and Slow Motion Shorty have all worn the noble crown of King of the Hoboes. Britt, Iowa, hosted its first hobo convention in 1900; from then until 1933 came a hiatus during which the town fathers tried to downplay Britt's reputation as hobo headquarters. In 1933, however, the town embraced its obvious destiny and conventions have been held there since (except during the war). As well as the election and coronation of King and Queen, the event also includes a 10k Hobo Run, a hobo art and talent show and a carnival. Hoboes march in their own parade,

followed by free mulligan stew for everyone. Hoboes from all around the United States travel to Iowa for the convention, where their ranks are swollen by thousands of spectators.

AUGUST. 3 days

Popcorn Festival

Van Buren, Indiana

Free
Contact: Popcorn Festival, 204 East Vine St., Van Buren, IN 46991

The 'popcorn center of the world' hosts a down-home festival to celebrate the abundance of this mildly explosive crop. Each year a long parade marches toward the crowning of the Popcorn Queen. Two other parades are held, one for babies and one for favorite family pets. Country music, square dancing and a teen dance are featured. The firemen hold a water ball contest; all helicopter rides are offered at the Little League field. Saturday night brings Popcorn Extravaganza entertainment, with a drawing for a $500 door prize. Over 90 booths are set up for the sale of delicious food, including the omnipresent popcorn, and homemade crafts.

AUGUST. 4 days

Village Art Festival

Amish Acres, Nappanee, Indiana

Admission
Contact: Amish Acres, 1600 W. Market, Nappanee, IN 46550

Puppetmakers and potters. . .ceramacists and carvers . . .weavers and wood turners. . .painters and photographers. . .dollcrafters and designers! Over 250 craftsmen annually show their wares at this historic farm. A re-creation of an 80-acre working farm, Amish Acres shows the beauty and industry of the plain people who homesteaded in area. Guided tours and horse-drawn buggy rides are available daily. The artists display in a market-like atmosphere around the farm pond. Marionettes, hand puppets, mimes, a juggler and an organ grinder with his monkey entertain the crowds, along with folk singers, gospel musicians and barbershop quartets. Visitors can wander through the farm, seeing the orchard or garden, the smokehouse, bake oven, blacksmith shop or windmill, and soak up a real feeling for farm life a hundred years ago. When hunger strikes, there are wagons of sausage sandwiches, lemonade, fudge, ice cream cones and fruit. The pig roast tent offers roast pork sandwiches, hamburgers, turkey legs and sweet corn. You'll also find a soda fountain, a fudgery and a family-style restaurant.

AUGUST. 5 days

Oahe Days

Pierre, South Dakota

Free
Contact: Pierre Area Chamber of Commerce, P.O. Box 548,
Pierre, SD 57501

Wacky contests, aquatic events and hometown fun characterize Oahe Days in South Dakota. A swim across the face of Oahe Dam is sponsored by the YMCA, a sailing regatta is held on Oahe Lake and in the evening houseboats and pontoons decorated with colorful flambeaux parade on the lake. Most of the contests appeal to children or betray a sense of humor, for instance, the bed making, frog jumping and shoe tying contests, the traditional three-legged race, the nose-propelled peanut push, family dog races and the nationally recognized, one-and-only Buffalo Chip Flipping Championship! You can enter the beer-drinking event, sweat in the triathlon, bicycle or road races, or join the Missouri River raft race. A beauty Queen is crowned and the band plays old-time music in the park.

MID-AUGUST THROUGH SEPTEMBER. 7 weekends

Minnesota Renaissance Festival

Shakopee, Minnesota

Admission charged.
Contact: Renaissance Festival, 3525 145th Street West,
Shakopee, MN 55379

Sixteenth century Europe is faithfully and joyfully re-created in Minnesota every summer. For seven busy weekends, a Renaissance village comes alive south of Shakopee. Peopled with over 500 costumed performers and craftsmen, the village re-creates the creativity and vitality of Europe's cultural awakening.

Performances occur on eight stages, and along the village's pathways as clowns buffoon, madrigals sing and poets recite. Visitors can feast on baked goods fresh from the ovens of village bakeries or choose hot meat direct from the open grills. A juried craft show is mounted and over 300 artists display and demonstrate their work. Jousting tournaments on horseback daily re-enact the the adventurous life of valiant knights. Contests and sporting events are open to all and include dueling for King of the Log, a Fight the Knight game, Elephant Rides, archery instruction and a turn on the Round-A-Bout. A falconer gives flying demonstrations of falcons and hawks. The Feast of Fantasy is staged twice daily in an English manor. Here guests are treated to a huge epicurean meal and several

theatrical and musical performances. King Henry and his courtiers, gypsies, peasants and wizards welcome the rollicking guests.

AUGUST/SEPTEMBER. 3 days

Balloon Races

Coshocton, Ohio

Free
Contact: Chamber of Commerce, P.O. Box 266, Coshocton,
OH 43812

The skies over Coshocton are filled with brilliant color as 30 balloons race this weekend. Every morning brings a flurry of activity at the fairgrounds as ground crews spread out the 70-foot balloons, untangle the lines and fire up the propane burners. The silent ascent takes place around 6:00 a.m. on morning launches, around 5:00 p.m. on evening launches. Pilots are instructed on the types of race to be flown just previous to their launch. The Balloonmeister determines the types of races and the targets. The balloonists must seek the favorable winds and navigate toward their targets. Viewers are welcome to the fairgrounds to watch the take off and the races. The grandstands are open and refreshments are available.

✳ *AUTUMN* ✳

LABOR DAY WEEKEND. 3 days

Santa-Cali-Gon Days

Independence, Missouri

Free
Contact: Chamber of Commerce, Box 147, Independence, MO
64051

What does Santa-Cali-Gon mean? Although this celebration has been running since 1940 and attracts

a quarter of a million visitors each year, there are still celebrants who wonder where the name came from. In the 1800's, Independence was the trailhead for three of the most famous overland trails to the West. Pioneers gathered supplies here, and wagon leaders organized wagon trains to trek along the Santa Fe, California, and Oregon trails.

Hence, the name. Santa-Cali-Gon Days harken back to the pioneer era with festivities centered around the square. Hundreds of artisans set up booths to sell and demonstrate many of the crafts basic to survival in the pioneer times. Local community groups sponsor food booths. Musical and theatrical groups perform at the grandstand, including The Three Trails Gang who re-enact many a bloody shootout. Visitors can view a fiddle contest, a twin contest, a pie-eating contest, a beard contest and the children's costume contest. Various bicycle and foot races are held, as well as a horseshoe pitching tournament and a checker tournament. A walk-race honoring Harry S. Truman will follow many of the paths the former president was fond of walking. During the week preceding Santa-Cali-Gon, a Treasure Hunt for a special festival medallion is held with clues to its location published in the local paper. The lucky finders of the medallion win a $500 prize.

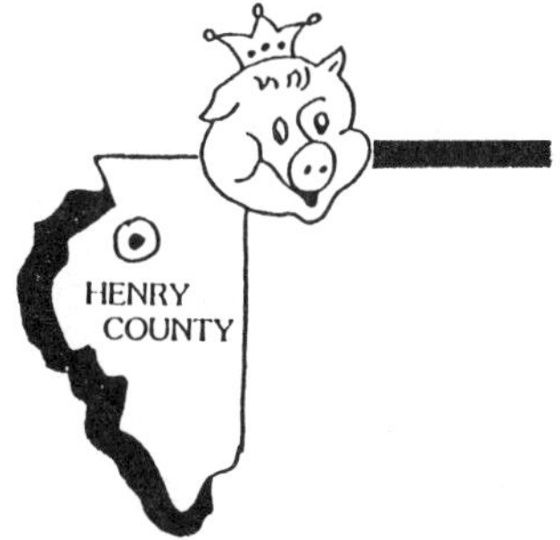

LABOR DAY WEEKEND. 3 days

Hog Capital of the World Festival

Kewanee, Illinois

Free
Contact: Hog Capital Festival Publicity, 310 E. Church St., Kewanee IL 61443

King Hog reigns in Kewanee, Illinois, and each Labor Day weekend the local citizens celebrate appropriately. A carnival is set up and events all over town affirm the emminence of pigs and pig products. The bemused visitor can shop at Hog Wild sales, run along in a four-mile Hog Jog, witness a Create-a-Pig contest, wander through a live hog exhibit, wallow in a mud volleyball tournament and, of course, pig out on ribs and pork chops. Tennis and golf tournaments are also held. This friendly midwestern festival also offers

such indigenous events as a hog calling contest, a pigtail contest and a tractor rodeo. Hogs and hospitality are both much in evidence in Kewanee this weekend.

Indian Princess contestants.

SEPTEMBER. 3 days

Fall Festival

Canaan, Indiana

Free
Contact: Canaan Restoration Council, Canaan, IN 47224

Each fall, Canaan hosts an old-fashioned celebration. The village is closed to traffic and visitors can reminisce about the horse-and-buggy days as they stroll the quiet, shady square. Arts and crafts booths and antique stalls invite the browser. Church stands sell baked goods, candies, jellies, Indian corn, pumpkins, sorghum, apple cider, quilts and other handmade goods. Saturday morning brings the Old-Fashioned Parade to the downtown streets.

Several unusual contests are staged during the festival. Eager contestants fatten up their frogs for the Heaviest Frog Contest, while others train more athletic frogs for the jumping events. Gourds are carefully measured and weighed for the largest, smallest and most unusual. Wood is sawed with a bucksaw in another contest. The stage is kept full of a variety of entertainment. Pretty girls enter an Indian Princess contest in homemade costumes. Everyone is invited to paint their rendition of the likeness of Chief White Eyes. The chief was a local Indian renegade held accountable for numerous scalpings. White Eyes' true history is lost to legend, but he is remembered in Canaan every fall as contestants try to recapture his fierce visage in their painting. A Pony Express mail run is held with the post office issuing a special cancellation in commemoration.

Popcorn Festival

Valparaiso, Indiana

Free

Contact: Chamber of Commerce, 601 E. Lincolnway, P.O. Box 330, Valparaiso, IN 46383

Pop on over to Indiana for a poppin' good time at the popular Popcorn Festival. Every September the hometown of Orville Redenbacher, father of gourmet popcorn, celebrates its main crop and the energy of its citizens. Events are varied, but most salute that fluffy, exploded kernel of corn. Festival day opens with a Popcorn Panic as entrants run five miles, then the kids get to run in the Little Kernel Puff. A carnival with games and kiddie rides is set up all day, and a gospel fest is held in the courthouse square. The Orville Redenbacher Popcorn tent is the site of talent shows, arts and crafts booths, food booths and square dancing. A grand parade with floats, music and a queen marches downtown.

Many pre- and post-festival activities are scheduled, most centered on sports events. The visitor can view a bicycle moto-cross, a criterium, the Popcorn Bowl football game, a pop-ball softball tournament, a national derby rally race, golf tournaments and other events. A popcorn art contest decorates downtown the week before the festival, and a grand Popcorn Ball with dinner, dancing and live entertainment kicks off the festivities.

Cedarburg Wine and Harvest Festival

Stone Mill Winery, Cedarburg, Wisconsin

Free

Contact: Wine and Harvest Festival, P.O. Box 204, Cedarburg, WI 53012

If you've ever felt the urge to stomp grapes barefooted, here's your chance. The historic town of Cedarburg, just 20 miles north of Milwaukee, holds a grape-stomping contest every year at the Wine and Harvest Festival. You don't have to be heavy to produce a lot of wine; so far the all-time festival champions have been members of the Milwaukee Ballet Company, known for their fancy footwork. This weekend features fun for the whole family, including clowns, musicians, an arts and crafts show, jousting matches staged by the Society for Creative

Anachronisms, a farmer's market and a gathering of homemade scarecrows.

In addition to the wine stomp, competitions are held in firewood splitting, chainsaw cutting and cherry pit spitting. So far, the local cherry pit spit record of 48 feet is a serious challenge to the world record. Great food is offered all weekend as the Cedarburg restaurants contribute their finest dishes to the harvest celebration. On Saturday evening a Fish Boil is held in the city park. Fish of all kinds, caught in local streams, are cooked up together in a huge, homemade stew.

Clog dancing.

SEPTEMBER. 2 days

Johnny Appleseed Anniversary Festival

Archer Park, Fort Wayne, Indiana

Free
Contact: Johnny Appleseed Anniversary Festival, 705 East State Blvd., Fort Wayne, IN 46805

Each year more than 250,000 visitors flock to Fort Wayne to celebrate the pioneer spirit of John Chapman, better known as Johnny Appleseed. Johnny was a colorful character of the Indiana frontier in the early 1800's, and spent his last years planting orchards in the Fort Wayne area. His gravesite is in Archer Park, where the festival takes place. The customs, entertainment, food, military life and Indian lore of the 1800's are displayed here. At craft booths you'll see costumed pioneers busily spinning, weaving, making soap, leather working and dulcimer

crafting. Indians demonstrate flint-knapping, basket weaving, leather crafting and wood working. Continuous free musical entertainment includes dulcimer playing, clog dancing and a fife-and-drum parade. Kids who want to be pioneers for a day can play Jacob's ladder, roll-the-hoop, tweezle-whop, or thread through staw mazes. Storytelling is also offered. The hungry will find ham and beans with stoneground cornbread. Fresh fruit and vegetables are available at the farmers' market. And there is a plentitude of apples, apples, apples!

MID-SEPTEMBER. 1 day

King Turkey Day

Worthington, Minnesota

Free
Contact: King Turkey Day, Inc., P.O. Box 310, Worthington, MN 56137

Since the Great Depression, turkeys have been the main crop around Worthington. This 'Turkey Capital of the World' attracts nationwide attention on its annual King Turkey Day. Political luminaries such as Lyndon Johnson, Robert Kennedy, Hubert Humphrey, Richard Nixon and Adlai Stevenson have addressed the local crowds as the TV networks and major print media record the festivities. The turkeys themselves have their moment of glory when they rush ahead of the big parade in cheerful flocks. The highlight of the festival is the Great Gobbler Gallop which pits a Worthington turkey against one from Cuero, Texas (another important turkey-raising area) in a mad race

for the three-foot tall Traveling Trophy of Tumultuous Triumph. In 1984, the local champ, 'Paycheck,' so named because he goes so fast, upheld Worthington's honor. The losing city is awarded the Circulating Consolation Cup of Consummate Commisseration, and another chance next year.

Octoberfest-Zinzinnati

Cincinnati, Ohio

Free
Contact: Downtown Council, 120 West Fifth St., Cincinnati, OH 45202

During the 1800's, the area around Cincinnati resembled the river valley of Rhineland with its rolling hills and vineyards. Many German immigrants settled here and their heritage is joyfully re-created each year in Octoberfest–Zinzinnati. Downtown Cincinnati is transformed into a Bavarian Alps village and Fifth Street is literally lined with dozens of booths featuring German specialities and the ubiquitous mug of beer. At Fountain Square the mayor formally taps the first keg and introduces the Gemutlichkeit Games where women can Sprint-for-a-Stein and men participate in the Beer Barrel Roll. Over two dozen musical groups are scheduled to appear, most of them such German dance bands as The Polka Dots or The Hot Brats. Festival-goers enthusiastically dance the traditional dances, occasionally quenching their thirst with a stein of special dark beer brewed by local breweries just for Octoberfest. Dancers and troubadors perform and a special Beer Barrel Roll-Off will be held for the media.

MID-SEPTEMBER in even-numbered years. 2 days

Cheese Days

Monroe, Wisconsin

Free
Contact: Cheese Days Inc., P.O. Box 606, Monroe, WI 53566

A quaint Old World style village nestled in the rolling hills of southern Wisconsin, Monroe is the 'Swiss Cheese Capital of the U.S.' Every other year this distinction is celebrated with a weekend of activities attracting more than 100,000 visitors. Entertainment, costumes and food are all Swiss-style. An arts and crafts show, one of the best in the Midwest, runs through the weekend. The Cheese Days Chase attracts runners to 10k and 20k events. The festival spirit of *gemutlichkeit*, defined as a combination of "geniality, coziness, hospitality, kind-

Demonstration of old-fashioned Swiss cheese making of a 200-lb. sheel in a copper kettle.

ness and good fellowship," continues in the children's Swiss costume parade around the square.

Entertainment includes yodeling, gymnastics, alpine horn blowing, flag throwing, singing and dancing. Swiss cheese making is demonstrated and a huge 200-pound wheel of Swiss is the center of the festival. A Cheesemakers Ball is held, as well as an exhibition of bands and street dancing. Sunday brings the Cheeseland Parade with over 200 units of floats and marching bands. Swiss specialty foods highlight the whole weekend, and you can sample cheeses and cheese sandwiches, homemade cream puffs, beer bratwurst, fried cheese curds and lots more.

OCTOBER. 3 days

Paul Bunyan Show

Nelsonville, Ohio

Admission charged
Contact: Paul Bunyan Show, Hocking Technical College, Route No. 1, Nelsonville, OH 45764

Paul Bunyan's mighty ax still bites deep into the timber of Ohio. Each year real-life lumbermen demonstrate their skills in Bunyanesque contests on the campus of Hocking Technical College. Climbing trees, balancing precariously on floating logs, felling timber and sawing mightily, these contestants celebrate the traditions of the logging industry. Not all events employ traditional skills; chainsaws and other modern technology are also used. Antique and contemporary logging equipment is displayed and demonstrated. Contests are held for both student and professional lumberjacks. Other festivities liven the scene. Ms Paul Bunyan is crowned Queen, chainsaw manufacturers demonstrate and auction wooden sculptures. In the evening a guitar playing contest is followed by square dancing. Hungry visitors can purchase a Bunyan Burger cooked over open flames to satisfy their larger-than-life appetites.

OCTOBER. 2 days

Covered Bridge Festival

Madison County, Iowa

Most events free
Contact: Chamber of Commerce, Box 55, Winterset, IA 50273

The seven covered bridges of Madison County cross not only the meandering waterways of the area, they also link the present with the pioneer era of the 1800's. Built by prudent decree of the country supervisors, these bridges protected horse riders and open carriages from winter storms. They are now the highlights of the Covered Bridge Festival as guided bus tours take visitors to view them during this celebration. Other events reminiscent of the 1880s include spelling bees, a fiddler's contest, horse races and a country music show. A local carpenter portrays Abe Lincoln in a storytelling performance. Contests include horseshoe pitching, muzzle loading and a marble tournament for the kids. Most events center around the courthouse lawn where local artisans in period costumes demonstrate and sell pioneer crafts. The visitor can see candle dipping, chair caning, sheep shearing, silver smithing, cider pressing, wool spinning, blacksmithing and the manufacture of other items basic to the times.

On Sunday afternoon a grand parade features marching bands and restored antique autos. An outlaw band roves the courthouse square 'robbing' the various craft and food booths until the sheriff and his boys finally round them up.

Feast of the Hunter's Moon

Fort Ouiatenon Historic Park, Lafayette, Indiana

Admission charged
Contact: Tippecanoe County Historical Assn., 909 South St., Lafayette, IN 47901

Fort Ouiatenon was the first fortified European settlement in Indiana. Established in 1717 by the French on the banks of the Wabash River, it provided a center for trade with the Indians and was a serious enough military threat to keep the British from the territory. Each year over 50,000 people return to the 1700s to spend a couple of days among the Indians, soldiers and traders in the Wabash Valley. One of the nation's outstanding historical festivals, the Feast is a re-creation of a gathering that might have occurred between the French and Indians at a fur-trading outpost 250 years ago. One secret of the Feast's success is its devotion to authenticity. More than 4,000 participants are carefully screened to make sure all details of costume, food, music and entertainment truly reflect life in the 18th century.

Feast is a full-family affair with lots of activities for the kids. Food includes Buffalo stew and Indian pudding. Craft demonstrations include broommaking, cornhusk weaving and pewter casting. Cannons are fired and tomahawks thrown. Pageants include a court martial, Indian dances, a Hueguenot worship service and the landing of the French *voyageurs*.

OCTOBER. 2 Saturdays

Fall Flyway

Fond du Lac, Wisconsin

Admission charged to bus tours
Contact: Convention & Visitors Bureau, 207 N. Main, Fond du Lac, WI 54935

Among the largest migrating birds, Canada geese annually fly south by tens of thousands in great V-shaped formations. Each fall they pass over Fond du Lac and pause at the Horicon marsh to rest and feed. During October, bus trips to the marsh are organized to view the birds. Audubon guides on the buses identify the birds and explain their habitat. Maps are also available for a drive-yourself tour of the area. Other harvest events occur this month as well. One orchard has hay rides to the pumpkin fields where you can pick your own jack-o-lantern. Local restaurants plan harvest dinners offering such delectable specialties as porky duck (duck with ribs), black swan (duck with raspberry sauce), and hot apple pie.

Stronghold Castle.

OCTOBER. 2 days

Autumn on Parade Festival

Oregon, Illinois

Admission charged to some events
Contact: Autumn on Parade, Box 234, Oregon, IL 61061

Join the pilgrimage to the beauties of the Rock River Valley, see a re-enactment of a Civil War encampment, tour the Stronghold Castle and watch the Harvest Time Parade, one of the Midwest's largest. Partake of an Olde English Dinner in the Rounde Room of the new Brubaker Center.

Oregon, Illinois, nestled at the foot of bluffs in the Rock River Valley, is noted for its hardwood forest. Hundreds of arts and crafts booths, and offerings of home-cooked food and breads will keep you fed and entertained. For the more ambitious, a Saturday morning 10k race or a two-mile fun run will open the day. Even if you're not a runner, it's interesting to watch striving bodies in action.

For the children, you'll find a space pillow, pony rides, cartoons, Three Stooges movies and pennies in the haystack. The whole family will enjoy greased pig chases, a pedal power pull and a cow milking contest. The Ogle County Historical Museum provides guided tours, and shouldn't be missed.

Circleville Pumpkin Show

Circleville, Ohio

Free
Contact: Circleville Pumpkin Show, 308 Northridge Rd.,
Circleville, OH 43113

Seeing is believing! The world's largest pumpkin pie, 350 pounds and five feet in diameter becomes the centerpiece to four days of celebration, involving seven parades, 50 bands, 40 floats and pumpkin delicacies galore: pumpkin-burgers, pumpkin waffles, pumpkin fudge, pumpkin donuts as well as pumpkin pie.

Join or watch the exuberant contests: hog calling, egg tossing, pie eating, big wheel racing, and the lovely contestants for the title of Miss Pumpkin and Little Miss Pumpkin. Six stages will be bustling with entertainment day and night. See clowns, jugglers, magicians, dancers, ventriloquists, guitarists and choirs.

Circleville calls this the 'Greatest free show on earth' and it certainly is a contender. The event has endured for 80 years and attracts more than 400,000 visitors to this small community each year.

Southwest

Boise City
Taos
Window Rock
Santa Fe
Claremore
Tulsa
Flagstaff
Gallup
Broken Arrow
Stroud
Oklahoma City
Albuquerque
ARIZONA
NEW MEXICO
OKLAHOMA
Quartzsite
Wickenburg
Phoenix
McKinney
Silver City
Fort Worth
Dallas
Tucson
Tombstone
Carlsbad
Deming
El Paso
TEXAS
Lufkin
Kerrville
Houston
San Antonio
Rockport

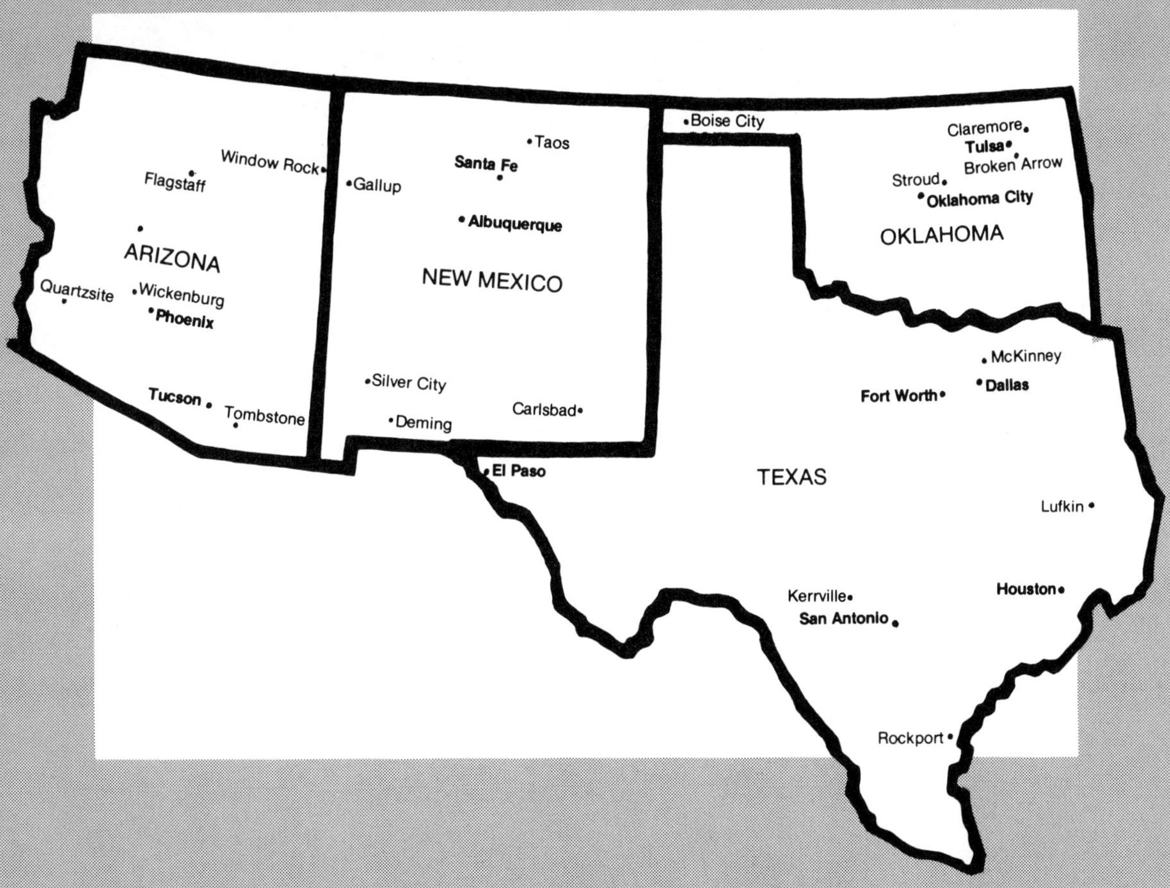

Music in the Park during the Houston Festival.

Duck Queen contestant in Deming, New Mexico.

Post-hole digging contest at Santa Fe Trail Daze.

Tucson Festival's Pioneer Days celebration.

Albuquerque International Balloon Fiesta.

The 1847 Kellum-Noble House, saved from destruction as the first act of the Society in 1954, is decorated with cedar and wreaths in a typical 19th century manner. Now located in a downtown Houston park, this home was for many years outside of Houston, although it is still in its original location.

DECEMBER. 3 days

Candlelight Tour of Sam Houston Park

Houston, Texas

Free
Contact: Harris County Heritage Society, 1100 Bagby, Houston, TX 77002

A nostalgic 19th century Christmas manages to occur in the midst of contemporary skyscrapers in downtown Houston. Ignoring this century, the public can view six Christmas celebrations in authentically restored, historic structures. Located in Sam Houston Park, each celebration is different and each typifies life in Texas as it was lived 150 years ago. An old cabin is simply decorated and presents a holiday feast with foods from Texas' forests and coastal waters. Here members of the Texas Army guard a watchfire, and periodically fire volleys of musket shots to commemorate the season. A country home visited by Santa is decorated in fine Victorian style. Dancers demonstrate the reels and quadrilles of the gentle folk in an urban house from the 1850s. One house is typical of the French Texans, complete with live harp music and a native Christmas tree. The German cottage is simpler, with a feast of German cooking and a native cedar surrounded by a miniature wooden village. St. John Church hosts the Singing Boys of Houston performing seasonal carols. Wassail is served to visitors and traditional Sand Tarts (holiday cookies) are sold. There are plans to expand the exhibits with the addition of an early 20th century house and a show from the Heritage Society's collection of antique toys.

FEBRUARY. 5 days

Quartzsite Pow Wow

Quartzsite, Arizona

Free
Contact: Quartzsite Improvement Association, Box 881, Quartzsite, AZ 85346

Agate, petrified wood, quartz crystals, jasper, fire agate, limonite cubes, opalite, calcite onyx, chalcedony roses, geodes, Apache tears, rhyolite and fossils. All are native to the Quartzsite area and can be found on local field trips, which makes this small desert community the perfect spot for a rockhound show and sale. What is so surprising is the size of the event. The town normally houses about 1,200 hardy souls, but during this week it may be visited by over a million vehicles. Rockhounds are a tenacious and curious group, and many live in areas where the winter climate makes a February trip to Arizona seem idyllic.

The Quartzsite Civic Center is the heart of all this activity. Hundreds of gem, jewelry, specimen and

THE "POW WOW"

QUARTZSITE, ARIZONA

fossil dealers offer their wares to hobbyists and professionals. Besides jewelry and mineral specimens, vendors offer lapidary equipment, jewelers' tools and other materials for sale. Visitors flock from all over America to browse for a special specimen, map or how-to advice on rockhounding. Field trips to local sites are conducted during the week. Most visitors camp in their own vehicles and the town offers ample trailer and RV accomodations. Nearby towns have motels and plenty of restaurants.

FEBRUARY. 3 days

Gold Rush Days

Wickenburg, Arizona

Admission charged to some events
Contact: Chamber of Commerce, Drawer CC, Wickenburg, AZ
85358

Precisely at 10 a.m., the Gold Shirt Gang shoots up the town of Wickenburg and then hangs the mayor, thereby officially opening Gold Rush Days. The local population of 4,000 swells to over 30,000 during this Old West celebration. The area is famous for the massacre of seven passengers on the Wickenburg stage in 1871. Attributed to local Indians, the slaughter gave the Army a good excuse to retaliate against the Apaches. This massacre is re-enacted

annually during the celebration. Other events include a three-day rodeo, country & western entertainment, gospel singing and a carnival. A large parade marches through the town. Contests include beard judging, mucking and drilling. The visitor can pan for gold and

Getting ready for the opening ceremony 'shoot-out.'

keep any he finds. An old-fashioned 'mellerdrama' is acted out nightly at the theatre. A big Cowboy Dance with country & western music is held at the community center as Wickenburg continues to celebrate the annual return of the Wild West.

Over 3,000 performing artists entertain in the parks and plazas of downtown as part of the Houston Festival. Here, the Houston Ballet presents 'Prince Igor' on one of the Festival's seven outdoor stages.

MID-MARCH. 10 days

The Houston Festival

Houston, Texas

Admission charged to some events
Contact: The Houston Festival, 1964 West Gray, Suite 227, Houston, TX 77019

All the bright spaces of Houston are filled each spring with a celebration of the arts. On weekends, seven stages present children's, classical and folk dance; country and pop; folk-ethnic; jazz-rhythm and Latin music. You can enjoy grand opera, a Broadway musical, the Houston Ballet, the Houston Symphony, big name bands and much more. Three markets tempt the visitor with unusual handmade and imported goods—the Juried Crafts and Arts Fair, the Gypsy Market and the International Market. Giant environmental sculptures decorate the green belt of Buffalo Bayou. Local museums hold special art, print and photography shows. Commissioned poets and prose writers read their works in Words Alive! Sky sculpture is launched, children parade in costumes, and the visitor can attend an art auction. Daily the towers and tunnels of Houston reverberate with music as concerts are held under the buildings and on the 60th floor of Texas Commerce Tower.

MARCH/APRIL. 3 days

Tucson Festival

Tucson, Arizona

Most events free
Contact: Tucson Festival Society, West Paseo Redondo,
Tucson, AZ 85719

The bang of Civil War re-enactments gets Pioneer Days off to an explosive start during Festival in Tucson. Mountain men hold muzzle-loading and tomahawk-throwing contests, while home cooking and frontier crafts are demonstrated. Pealing bells and brilliant fireworks herald the birthday of San Xavier Mission. Visitors can shop for dinner from one of the Indian food booths and watch the Indian and folkloric dancing. Hundreds of children dress up in home-made costumes for the Fiesta de los Ninos parade, and afterwards are entranced by clowns. Festival's final event is a huge gathering of amateur and professional mariachi groups. Free concerts are offered around the city, and dedicated mariachi patrons can hire a band for special events.

APRIL AND SEPTEMBER. Last weekends

Bird Migration Weekends

Silver City, New Mexico

Charges for accomodations and tours

Experienced birdwatchers consider southwest New Mexico a birding hot spot. Resident species are unique, unlike those in other sections of the United States, with Mexican species frequently visiting. However, the most exciting birdwatching occurs during the spring and fall migrations as thousands of birds negotiate their ancestral flyways either to or from their nesting grounds. In the spring, visitors to New Mexico can spot warblers, grosbeaks, orioles, flycatchers and hummingbirds returning to this country from their winter in Central or South America. In fall, sparrows and wrens can also be seen as they traverse thousands of miles heading south again. In April and September, the Bear Mountain Guest Ranch offers special tours of the area to seek these birds. A naturalist guides the tours and provides bird lists. Birders from as far away as Canada travel here to add to their life lists of species spotted.

LATE APRIL. 10 days

Fiesta San Antonio

San Antonio, Texas

Free
Contact: Fiesta San Antonio Commission, 1145 E. Commerce
St., San Antonio, TX 78205

A giant ten-day, multicultural celebration explodes in San Antonio each April. Organized almost a century ago, Fiesta originally honored famous Texas heroes. Over the decades it has expanded to include all the diverse elements of the community and now features over 150 events located in every corner of the town, including several military bases and posts in the area. Uniquely Texan, Fiesta blends Mexican, German, Irish, French, Jewish, English and American elements in a glorious cascade of events.

Four great parades highlight Fiesta, starting with the Parade of the Ugly King *(Del Rey Feo)*, continuing with a Battle of Flowers Parade, a parade on the river with floats that really float, and a giant, illuminated night parade through the streets. Events around town will attract art lovers, cactus fans, historic photograph collectors, runners, *mariachi* lovers, balloon racers, rugby and soccer enthusiasts, and all who delight in fireworks displays. Ethnic food lovers can find almost all their favorites here: baked oysters, New Orleans specialties, a *mercado* stuffed with Mexican treats, hot dogs and representative dishes of many other cuisines. Queens are crowned, fashions are shown, music sounds in many quarters, historically clad ballgoers dance the night away as confetti flurries through the air. An authentic Mexican rodeo highlights the final day of festivities.

One of the largest and more varied of America's festivals, Fiesta in San Antonio is celebrated by nearly five million participants each year, and is getting bigger.

MAY. 1 day

May Fair

McKinney, Texas

Free
Contact: Chamber of Commerce, P.O. Box 621, McKinney, TX 75069

Experience the nostalgic charms of a simple country

festival at May Fair. Time seems to have stopped long before the twentieth century at this annual McKinney celebration. The fair grounds behind the courthouse are converted into a village of booths where the visitor can find arts, crafts and antiques to buy. Singers, dancers, puppeteers, clowns and musicians delight the crowds. There are a variety of game booths, including contests of paper airplane folding, bubble gum blowing, beard growing and dancing. Local cooks can enter a baked goods contest, and the athletic can compete in horseshoe pitching, three-legged or sack races. The garden club stages its annual flower show at the library. Young dancers in costume

perform a traditional dance around the May Pole three times a day accompanied by live Baroque music. The beautifully restored antique houses around Chestnut Square are open for tours all day. Festivities conclude with a street dance around the square in the evening.

MAY. 2 days

Rooster Days

Broken Arrow, Oklahoma

Free
Contact: Chamber of Commerce, 123 North Main, Broken Arrow, OK 74012

There aren't many roosters left in Broken Arrow's festival, but in the 1930s they were the focus of the whole weekend. Back then, local farmers were trying to increase their egg busines, and the best way to do this was by culling the roosters. With the roosters gone, the hens laid infertile eggs which lasted much longer and brought a better price on the market. So, once a year the roosters were brought to town and sold by the ton. Gradually a celebration built up around the weekend, and it continues to this day featuring a big carnival and exhibits in arts and crafts booths. Local singers and bands perform alongside professional groups. The main event is a big parade on Saturday. Filled with clowns, bands, floats, horses and dignitaries, the parade even has a token rooster, in reality a human dressed up in fake feathers. A Pioneer Dinner is held for those who have lived in Broken Arrow for more than fifty years, the folk who remember the real roosters!

Southern Hushpuppy Olympics and Forest Festival

Lufkin, Texas

Admission charged
Contact: Visitor and Convention Bureau, P.O. Box 1606,
Lufkin, TX 75901

In eastern Texas, hushpuppy cooking is considered such a vital part of life that it deserves its own Olympic-style competition. Hushpuppy chefs, usually in bizarre costumes, prepare their best recipes in hopes of winning the $1,000 prize. The drama of the proceedings is heightened by another cash award for showmanship, and it is not uncommon to see cooks in prison attire or dressed up as a corn cob, jalapeno pepper or green onion. The Hushpuppy Olympics is only one event of the annual Forest Festival.

There is also an extensive arts and crafts show sponsored by the Museum of East Texas. A parade through downtown Lufkin officially opens the celebration. A lumberjack show presents championship displays of log rolling, axe throwing, log burling and relay racing. Rural fire departments from Angelina County compete in various events. Representatives of the forest industry exhibit equipment and products. Children love the carnival and petting zoo. And everyone, whose appetite is awakened by the sight and smell of cooking hushpuppies, will appreciate the wide selection of food booths.

Mayfest

Tulsa, Oklahoma

Admission charged to some events
Contact: Arts and Humanities Council, 2210 S. Main St.,
Tulsa, OK 74114

Mayfest is a huge celebration of the arts, bringing 130 juried artists and craftsmen, 120 performers on six stages and 30 international food vendors to Tulsa's downtown Main Mall. Over 500,000 people attend this celebration of spring, some to hear the music, some to taste the delicious food, some to view the arts and others to try their hand at participatory art booths. Special events have included the Woody Guthrie Tribute, a special Night of Mayfestivity with 35 top artists, a singer and songwriter competition, symphony performances and cajun, country, blues, folk, celtic and jazz music.

MAY/JUNE. 2 consecutive weekends

Texas Arts & Crafts Fair

Kerrville, Texas

Admission charged
Contact: Texas Arts & Crafts Foundation, P.O. Box 1527,
Kerrville, TX 78028

Brightly colored tents and shady oaks dot the fairgrounds in Kerrville. A small creek winds through rolling hills and down into the fair, bales of hay are stacked in the shade to provide impromptu seating for festival-goers. Over 200 artistans display and demonstrate their crafts. Collectors watch for new talent and buy from seasoned craftspeople. A Pioneer Village features handcrafts from an earlier era as well as blacksmithing, soap making, pioneer cooking and yarn making. Over 30 food booths sell many specialties including chicken fried steak sandwiches and such Mexican favorites as tamales, fajitas and chalupas. Musicians and dancers perform on two stages, everything from country-western to bluegrass and classical. Folk singers and clowns stroll around the fairgrounds to everyone's delight. Children will be entertained in their own area by a petting zoo, hands-on crafts corner, a storyteller and a magician. A well-attended event, this celebration brightens Memorial Day and the following weekend every year.

JUNE. 4 days

Santa Fe Trail Daze

Boise City, Oklahoma

Most events free
Contact: Chamber of Commerce, Box 1027, Boise City, OK
73933

In the early 1800s, thousands of pioneers trekked along the Santa Fe trail, following wagon ruts to a new life in the West. Part of the trail cut through Cimarron County in the panhandle of Oklahoma where the people of Boise City now commemorate the long and hazardous journey of those adventurers. Free bus tours of county historical spots are available. Most of the sites are on private land and are offered for public viewing only at this time. Included are visits to Autograph Rock where early travelers scratched their names and dates on a sandstone cliff, a ghost town, fossilized dinosaur tracks imbedded in a creek bottom, the three-cornered meeting place of New Mexico, Colorado and Oklahoma, a bandit hide-out, rock pinnacles curiously shaped by erosion into heads, and a section of the actual Santa Fe trail showing the deep path cut by wagon wheels and pack animals.

The festival includes many more events, most of them frontier oriented—a western musical with local talent, a junior rodeo, buggy rides, square dances, a cakewalk and an oldtime fiddling contest. Visitors may attend a free watermelon feed or pancake breakfast, shop at the Flea Market, watch a posthole digging contest or attend the dance. Saturday brings a parade entitled 'Our Notorious Past' with prizes for those who best depict the yesteryears of an area once called 'No Man's Land.'

LAST FULL WEEKEND IN JUNE. 3 days

New Mexico Arts and Crafts Fair

Albuquerque, New Mexico

Admission charged
Contact: New Mexico Arts and Crafts Fair, 2745 San Mateo,
NE Suite G, Albuquerque, NM 87110

An important cultural event in the Southwest, New Mexico's unique arts and crafts are displayed in a traditional, open-air market. All exhibitors are residents of New Mexico, and their wares include fiber arts, all different media of painting, pottery, jewelry, photography, stained glass, beadwork, enamelware, folk sculpture, fine art prints, handmade paper, leather goods and much more. Rigorous selection procedures guarantee work of the highest quality. The visitor can also select regional foods, enjoy live entertainment, or watch craft demonstrations while the children are treated to puppet shows and face painting. A special exhibit of local children's art is also mounted.

JUNE/AUGUST. 8 weeks

Taos Chamber Music Festival

Taos, New Mexico

Admission charged
Contact: Taos School of Music, Box 1879, Taos, NM 87571

For decades picturesque Taos has been a magnet for artists of all persuasions. Here, the oldest chamber music program in the country offers an eight-week program of concerts and lectures each summer. Performances are by the professional staff of the School of Music and are scheduled for Saturday nights. A series of student concerts are also held at Hotel St. Barnard in the Sangre de Cristo mountains above Taos. Faculty members of the School are distinguished musicians, and their students have gone on to join some of the major chamber groups and orchestras throughout the world. Each summer thousands of visitors to Taos eagerly await this series of concerts.

JULY. 1 day.

International Brick & Rolling Pin Throw

Stroud, Oklahoma

Free
Contact: Chamber of Commerce, Stroud, OK 74079

Four towns named Stroud grace the English-speaking world, one each in Oklahoma, Ontario, Gloucestershire, and New South Wales. Each year they compete in brick and rolling pin throws. The original contest

started in Oklahoma as a celebration of the brick manufacturing industry there. It grew to include the other towns of Stroud, and the rolling pin event was added so women would have a chance to compete. Also, Stroud in New South Wales boasts a rolling pin factory. The male competitors in each of the towns throw a five-pound brick, while the women heave a two-pound pin. Records and results are carefully tabulated over the phone, and International Champions become eligible to compete in the Champion of Champions. To help the community get in the right spirit for this serious athletic event, downtown merchants hold a sale and a parade prior to the actual 'throw-offs.'

Hopi and Navajo Craftsman Exhibitions

Flagstaff, Arizona

Admission charged
Contact: Museum of Northern Arizona, Route 4, Box 720,
Flagstaff, AZ 86001

By the late 1920s, many Native American crafts were no longer practiced and collectors showed little interest in these art forms. Concerned by this decline, the co-founder of the Museum of Northern Arizona organized the first Hopi Craftsman Exhibition in 1930. Its success stimulated the Museum to establish a parallel exhibit for the Navajos. These two exhibitions are the premier events in the Museum's month-long Festival of Native American Arts. Collectors and artists from all around the country travel to Flagstaff to view these exhibits. The Hopi Exhibition will show more than 1,000 items including Kachina dolls, rattles, plaques, paintings, jewelry, pottery and weavings. Rugs are the highlights of the Navajo exhibit and many outstanding styles are shown. Also included are baskets, pots, jewelry and painting. Cash prizes are awarded to each division and these winners are exhibited in the Special Exhibits gallery. Visitors will enjoy the native artisans who demonstrate their arts and crafts in the Museum patio. A variety of Indian foods will be on sale, too.

Inter-Tribal Indian Ceremonial

Red Rock State Park, Gallup, New Mexico

Admission charged
Contact: Inter-Tribal Indian Assn., P.O. Box 1, Church Rock,
NM 87311

Campfires of friendship have been lit every August for over 50 years as Indians from all over the country gather in New Mexico's red rock country to celebrate inter-tribal harmony. This festive celebration has always been considered an educational event, where non-Indians could see the best of Indian culture. Today, with Indian youths losing their cultural affiliations, the Ceremonial also serves to remind Native

Americans of their tribal traditions. Throughout the days, the festival features informal demonstrations of dances, games and ceremonials. In the evenings more formal programs of Indian activities take place in the amphitheatre. The dances are completely authentic in costume, music and detail. On Saturday morning, an all-Indian parade marches in full costume through downtown Gallup. An Indian rodeo, co-sanctioned by Indian cowboy associations, is run each day with all the major rodeo events. The art exhibit at Ceremonial is sought out by worldwide collectors of Indian art. Indian artists believe that art is a natural expression of being, and some of the country's finest native artists exhibit and sell here. Included are such traditional Indian art forms as jewelry, weavings, pottery, baskets, wood carvings, painting, sculpture and beadwork.

Karen Jaceldo of the Philippine Dance Ensemble gracefully portrays tales of courtship and celebration found in Filipino folk dances at the Texas Folklife Festival in San Antonio.

AUGUST. 4 days

Texas Folklife Festival

San Antonio, Texas

Admission charged
Contact: University of Texas, Institute of Texan Cultures at
San Antonio, P.O. Box 1226, San Antonio, TX 78294

Celebrating Texas' rainbowed ethnic background, this event draws enormous crowds each year. Pioneer

skills demonstrated include soap making, sheep shearing, corn shucking, goose plucking and blacksmithing. Visitors will be amazed at the number and variety of ethnic groups cooking specialty foods for sale. Where else could you savor Korean pickled cabbage, Hungarian goulash, Filipino egg rolls, Cajun gumbo, Welsh cake, Mexican tacos, Irish stew, Czech sausage, pickled pigs' feet and dozens of others?

Sponsored by the University of Texas Institute of Texan Cultures, The Texas Folklife Festival helps perpetuate all the varied traditions that make up the state. The music is endless and curious contests like watermelon seed spitting, crawfish racing and arm wrestling are delightful to behold.

LATE AUGUST. 3 days

The Great American Duck Race

Deming, New Mexico

Free
Contact: Chamber of Commerce, P.O. Box 3, Deming, NM
88031

A 'flock' of infamous racers gather in Deming each summer for the annual running of the Duck Races. Heats pit such entrants as 'Bird in a Fist' against

'Quack Power' and 'Yacky Qacky.' The Duck Races are run each afternoon on Saturday and Sunday. However, the festivities go far beyond the main events. Ducks also compete in the Best Dressed Duck Contest. Friday evening a Duck Queen is chosen from appropriately costumed lovelies, and a Duck Queen Ball is held to the tunes of a country band. Saturday morning sees a mass ascent of hot air balloons, followed by the Great American Duck Race Parade. Contestants can win cash prizes in the horseshoe tournament and the world's richest Tortilla Toss. Originated in 1980, the Deming Duck Races have matured into one of the country's most prestigious sporting events.

❋ *AUTUMN* ❋

Miss Navajo Nation.

Navajo Nation Fair

Window Rock, Arizona

Admission charged
Contact: Navajo Tribe, P.O. Box Drawer U, Window Rock, AZ 806515

The dramatically beautiful Southwest desert is home to the Navajo nation, which holds its annual celebration at Window Rock. Named for the giant hole eroded in the sandstone formations, this Arizona town is the Navajo cultural center. Besides the fair, a Navajo tribal museum, a zoological park and botanical garden are located here. Jewelry, rugs and other native crafts are displayed at the arts and crafts booths. Fry bread is cooked over hot cedar coals; mutton stew and Navajo tacos are sold. An International Pow Wow brings participants from more than sixty different tribes. Traditional Navajo dancing and singing is presented every evening. An Indian Rodeo is held every day. Navajo agriculture and commerce are exhibited. Miss Navajo is crowned Queen. And every evening the desert air resounds to concerts by leading rock groups and country singers.

OCTOBER. 9 days

Albuquerque International Balloon Fiesta

Albuquerque, New Mexico

Admission charged at launch site
Contact: Albuquerque International Balloon Fiesta, Inc., 4804 Hawkins NE, Albuquerque, NM 87109

Each fall Albuquerque celebrates the simple fact that hot air rises with the spectacular launching of over 500 hot air balloons. The self-styled capital of hot air ballooning plays host to this colorful nine-day event. Balloonists from all over the country bring their equipment and climb the air waves in brilliantly colored spheres. Once aloft, pilots maneuver in the currents to compete in World-Class Gas Balloon

Championships. A variety of other competitions are also held, including a race where pilots drop a projectile (often the humble tumbleweed) from the air onto a target and another race where 'coyote' pilots try to out-maneuver 'roadrunner' pilots through the tricky air currents. Hot air ballooning requires mild winds, lots of sunshine and ample space, all of which characterize Albuquerque. This colorful, air-born celebration is attended by over half a million visitors each year.

MID-OCTOBER. 3 days

Helldorado

Tombstone, Arizona

Free
Contact: Chamber of Commerce, P.O. Box 297, Tombstone AZ
85638

Tombstone's violent past is re-created in these three days. Melodramas portraying such classic Old West confrontations as the Bisbee Massacre and the Gunfight at the O.K. Corral are re-enacted by the now-peaceful citizens of 'The Town Too Tough To Die.' Tombstone in the late 1800s was a rip-roaring silver mining town, where most arguments and power clashes were solved with hot lead showered from six-shooters. Every October cowboys, sheriffs, saloon girls, bartenders and outlaws clash again in dramatic enactments.

MID-OCTOBER THROUGH MID-APRIL. Tuesdays through Sundays

Whooping Crane Tours

Rockport, Texas

Admission charged
Contact: Capt. Ted Appell, Star Route 1, Box 225J, Rockport,
TX 78382

As we near the end of the twentieth century, it is clear that many of America's wildlife species won't survive much longer. Other populations, however,

reached the brink of extinction only to be brought back by careful wildlife management. The Whooping Crane is a good example of this; down to 14 survivors in the late 1930s, there are now more than 80 birds in the latest count, and their numbers are expected to increase. These birds winter in Aransas National Wildlife Refuge on the gulf coast of Texas. The motor vessel 'Whopping Crane' runs daily tours of the marshy estuaries to view the local wildlife. Besides the cranes, approximately 200 other species of birds can be spotted here, along with deer, javalina, armadillos and snakes. During the fall Canadian Geese arrive, along with many other kinds of waterfowl. Sandhill Cranes winter in the reserve and the rare Caracara lives here permanently. Birdwatchers from all over the country arrive to add to their life lists. The boat is equipped with a large sundeck, lounge, snack bar and rest rooms. It conducts the only scheduled daily tour through 40 miles of the Aransas Refuge.

NOVEMBER. 1 day

Bat Flight Breakfast

Carlsbad Caverns, Carlsbad, New Mexico

Admission charged
Contact: National Park Service, Carlsbad Caverns, 3225
National Parks Highway, Carlsbad, NM 88220

Breakfast with the bats is an eerie and exciting event in New Mexico. For thousands of years bats have used an upper portion of the Carlsbad Caverns for summer roosting. The bats winter in Mexico and return to Carlsbad each year to give birth to their babies and nurse them to adulthood. Every evening the bats leave the caves in great swirling flights of 5,000-10,000 animals. They are nocturnal and spend the night feeding on flying insects. By morning they return to the caves to rest another day. Their re-entry into the caves is an amazing spectacle. They fold their wings and dive at the entrance to the caves at great speeds. In this headlong rush, their wings vibrate and set up a strange sound—an echoing vibration that grows with the number of bats coming in. Many visitors have seen the bats spiral out of the caves in the evening, but few have seen them plummet back in. The park service initiated a special breakfast to encourage visitors to witness the bats' precipitous trajectory. Breakfast is served near the entrance to the caverns and early-birds can watch the early-bats rushing home to sleep.

Actually, if it weren't for the bats, no one would know of Carlsbad Caverns. It was the sight of the bats exiting in great clouds that first drew settlers to the cavern. The discovery of the bats led soon to the mining of their guano. It is estimated they have been

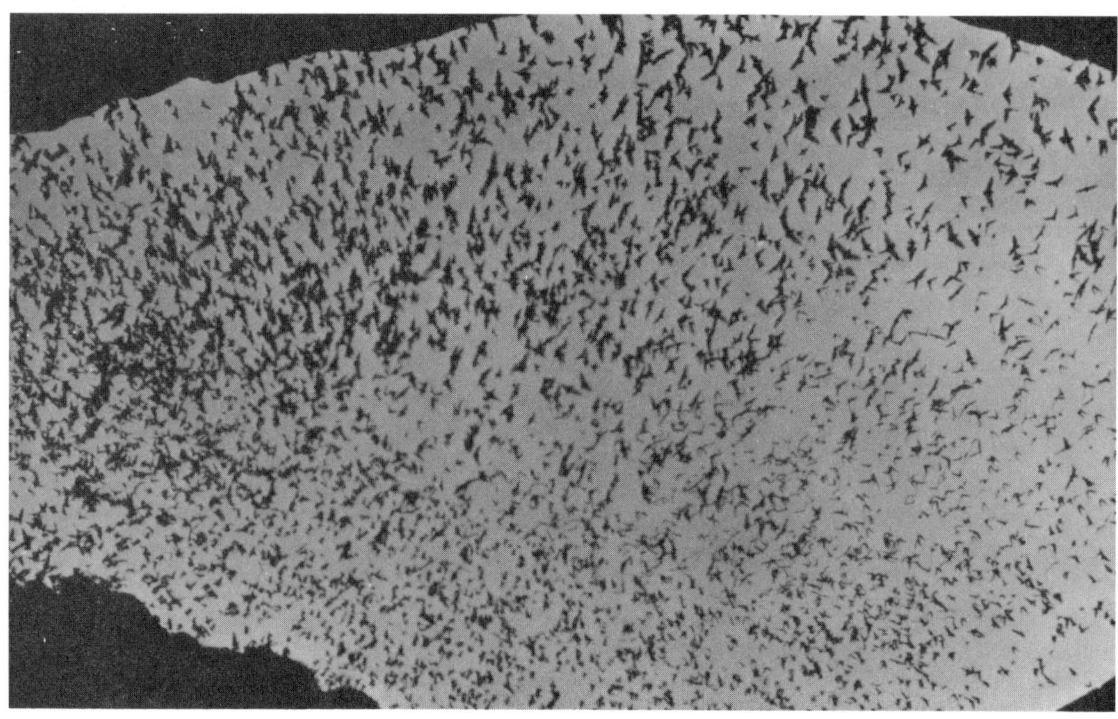

using the caves for over 17,000 years, so a commercially large store of guano had accumulated. One hundred thousand tons were removed in just twenty years. It was a foreman for one of the guano companies who explored the full extent of the caverns and his interest helped them gain national monument status. The bat population is considerably smaller now, but the Mexican Freetail bats continue to migrate here and provide a fascinating glimpse into the habits of this little known mammal.

NOVEMBER. 4 days

Will Rogers Day

Claremore, Oklahoma

Admission charged only for Birthday Supper and Dance.
Contact: Will Rogers Memorial, P.O. Box 157, Claremore, OK 74018

America's greatest homegrown humorist liked to brag that his family didn't come over on the *Mayflower*, instead they met it at the dock when it landed. Of Indian descent, Rogers' charm and humor won him friends across the country, from the White House to the working man. Involved in the early years of aviation development, he died in a tragic plane crash at the age of 44.

Part Cherokee, Rogers was born in Oklahoma and each year his hometown celebrates his birthday with a four-day festival. A Country Fair with displays of local craftsmen, square dancing and a flea market is held each day. The event opens with a Pioneer Breakfast with participants costumed in frontier get-ups. A Birthday Party on Saturday morning is held at the Roger's birthplace, with free cake and punch, a band, family members, speakers and an air show. A Birthday Supper is given on Monday evening with barbecue and entertainment, including an auction to benefit the Friends of Will Rogers Memorial Library. Will Rogers movies are run throughout the festival, with chili cook-offs, gospel singing and various sports events coinciding. The festival concludes with a memorial wreath-laying and a reception to honor Rogers' enduring place in American history.

A birthday cake is served at the Oologah birthplace to commemorate the 100th birthday of Will Rogers in 1979.

Rocky Mountain

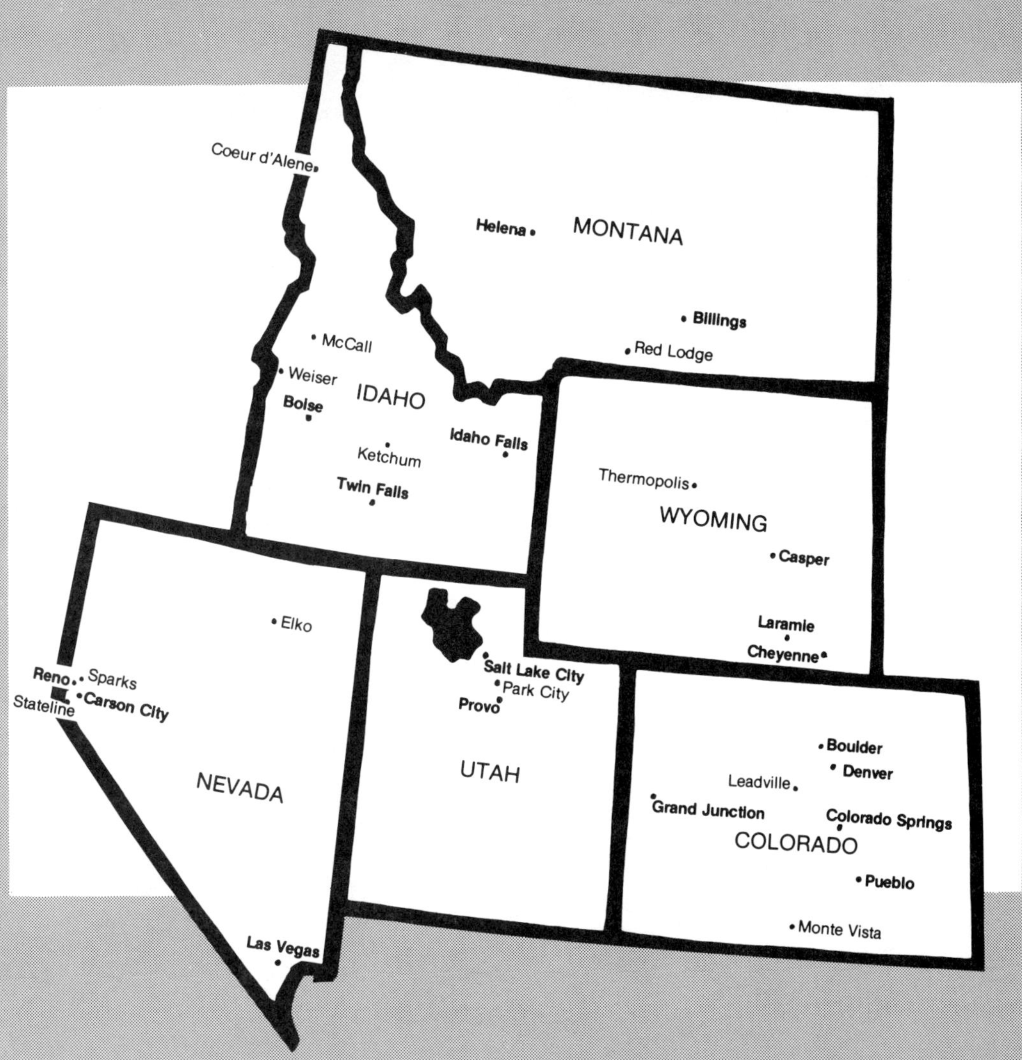

A taste of summer in the Rocky Mountains.

Park City Art Festival.

Art on the Green, Coeur d'Alene, Idaho.

Great High Sierra Chili Cook-Off.

DECEMBER. 1 day

A Victorian Christmas

Leadville, Colorado

Admission charged
Contact: Chamber of Commerce, Box 861, Leadville, CO
80461

Leadville's grande dames are a collection of Victorian homes built at the end of the last century. Lovingly restored and decorated by their present owners, they are the center of this holiday celebration. The homes are open all afternoon with costumed guides showing the highlights of the houses and serving hors d'oeuvres and punch. Dinner follows at the 'Old Church' Arts and Humanities Center with a meal catered by a famous local restaurant. Diners are entertained by carolers in Victorian attire. After dinner, a local opera troupe presents a program of traditional Christmas music and selections from an opera based on the saga of one of Colorado's legendary Silver Kings. Dessert is served during intermission. Built in the heyday of Leadville's mining boom, these homes represented wealth and respectability to their owners. Today they are a charming reminder of elegant craftsmanship and a beautiful setting for these holiday festivities.

JANUARY. 12 days

National Western Stock Show

Denver, Colorado

Admission charged
Contact: National Western Stock Show, 1325 E. 46th Ave.,
Denver, CO 80216

The largest livestock show on the continent takes place in Denver each January. Over half a million people attend and the dollar value of livestock changing hands is staggering—$10,000,000 worth and 15,000 individual animals exhibited. But statistics can't describe the event or its importance to the western cattle industry. Founded in 1906, the livestock judging and sales remain the very foundation of this festival, with many associated contests and judgings. For instance, there is a Fed Beef Contest to judge the quality of dressed carcasses; an auction of champion steers, lambs and hogs; and a Sheep Shearing Contest. A Horse Show is held, with events on each day of the event.

For youngsters, several 4-H contests are staged. A

professional rodeo takes place with cowboys from all over America competing. A Petting Zoo delights younger show-goers, as well as a trained buffalo show, draft horse exhibit and events involving horses no bigger than dogs. A replica of a stagecoach, pulled by a team of six perfectly matched quarter-horses, races around the stadium in a demonstration of pioneer transportation. Youth riding groups perform synchronized routines. Mules and draft horses have pulling contests. A Rodeo Queen is chosen to reign over the entire celebration.

FEBRUARY. 10 days

Winter Carnival

McCall, Idaho

Most events free
Contact: Chamber of Commerce, P.O. Box D, McCall, ID
        83638

It isn't easy to sculpt a whale, a dragon, a clown or anything else from ice. After artist and crew pack sufficient snow to make a base, the hard work begins. Snow and water are mixed to make slush, which is then piled slowly into shape. Details are etched with the appropriate tools, and more slush is kept handy to add to the work. When finished, the piece must be sprayed every night to encourage a fine icy glaze. Also, any snow accumulating must be

carefully brushed off. The artists and crew get wet and cold, and the sculpture survives only if the weather cooperates. But, despite the effort, the ice sculptures are the heart of McCall's winter festivities. McCall is in the middle of a large winter recreation area so, naturally, their celebration features all sorts of winter sports—snowmobile races, cross country ski races, telemark races, downhill skiing, sleigh rides, and even ski movies for the sedentary. A Torchlight Parade is held the first evening in downtown, along with the announcement of the winners in the Ice Sculpture Contest. There is even a Snowman Building Contest for the youngsters. Over 30 food booths offer regional and foreign specialities for the hungry visitor. And, watching over all the festivities are the silent, frozen grins of the ice sculptures.

JUNE. 1 week

National Oldtime Fiddlers' Contest

Weiser, Idaho

Admission charged
Contact: Chamber of Commerce, 8 East Idaho, Weiser, ID 83672

Fiddlers entertain pioneers crossing the Great Plains in wagon trains. On the frontier, they fiddled their tunes in mining camps and saloons. As towns replaced the camps, they resined their bows for hoedowns and square dances. The National Oldtime Fiddlers' Contest helps to preserve the art of fiddling as well as keeping the oldtime tunes alive. The contest develops new audiences for this music, and encourages young musicians to learn the old techniques and music.

Cash prizes and trophies are offered in seven categories—senior, ladies, men's, junior, junior-junior, small fry and accompanists. Contests are held during the week, and Saturday is the grand finale with a big Oldtime Parade. Everyone is encouraged to wear oldtime western dress and parade entries usually exhibit relics and mementoes of the past. A barbecue in the park is held after the parade. During this week, musicians stage impromptu jam sessions and performances. Saturday night draws the biggest crowds as the Grand Champion Finals are held and the top awards presented.

LATE JUNE. 1 week

Reno Rodeo

Reno, Nevada

Admission charged
Contact: Reno Rodeo & Livestock Association, Inc., P.O. Box 12335, Reno, NV 89510

This *Wildest and Richest* rodeo in the West, jewel in the crown of the Rodeo Capital of the World, has been nominated as one of the 'Top 100' events in the U.S. by the American Businessmen's Association. Featuring the second largest prize money in North American, the Reno Rodeo draws cowboys and professional rodeo champs from all over the country. Approximately 100,000 people attend the rodeo and its associated events.

A Frontier Village, complete with entertainment,

chuckwagon, and a nightly dance, shares the rodeo grounds. Downtown Reno hosts both a western art fair and a craft exposition, as well as an antique equestrian equipment auction and a huge carnival. The Rodeo and other events re-create the wild and wooly heritage of the West and should please the cowboy hiding in everyone's heart.

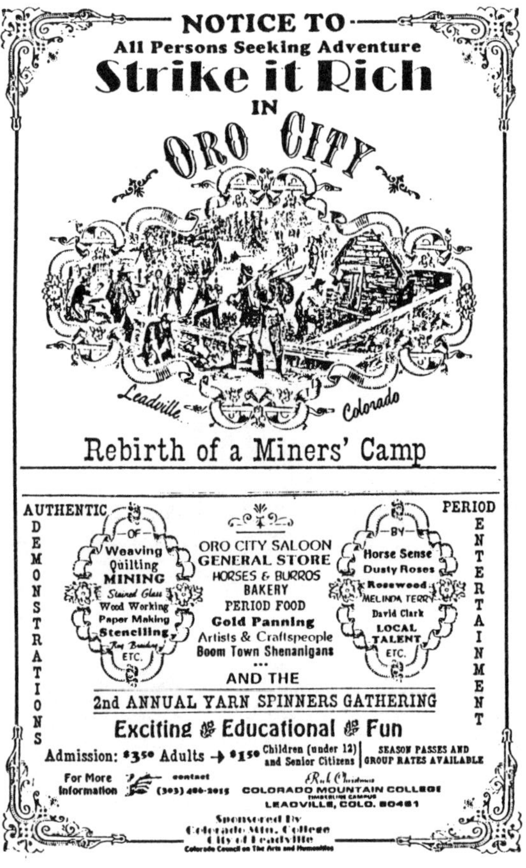

JUNE/JULY. 9 days

Oro City: Rebirth of a Miner's Camp

Leadville, Colorado

Admission charged
Contact: Chamber of Commerce, P.O. Box 861, Leadville, CO 80461

In the 1800s, the original Oro City was composed of "scattered cabins, tents, bough huts, wagons with people living in and under them, and saloons." A rip-roaring mining camp built to serve the gold miners, Oro City gradually evolved into the modern city of Leadville.

Every summer, Colorado Mountain College and Leadville bring Oro City to life again. Entertainers, yarnspinners, artists and craftspeople inhabit this colorful camp. Classes and demonstrations are held in pioneer crafts and skills such as doll making, rug braiding, paper making, blacksmithing, weaving, wood carving, quilting, assaying, woodstove baking, mining and panning, goldsmithing and beer brewing. Performers appear in the saloon and on stage delighting the audience with authentic songs, narratives and humor from the gold mining era. Professional story-tellers entertain at the Yarnspinners Gathering, with stories, poetry and music. A general store and a bakery dispense oldtime food. Curious visitors can even try their hand at panning for gold. On the 4th of July, a large parade will be held in downtown Leadville. The final night of Oro City brings a benefit auction where the goods created by the resident artists and craftpeople are sold to help support next year's event.

JULY 4TH WEEKEND. 3 days

Dixieland Jazz Festival

Sparks, Nevada

Admission charged
Contact: Nugget, P.O. Box 797, Sparks, NV 89431

New Orleans comes to the desert every 4th of July weekend when the Nugget hosts its Dixieland Jazz Festival. Ten renowned jazz bands from around the country perform all weekend in three different in-house locations. The bands play on a rotating basis so you won't miss a single one during this syncopated weekend. Impromptu sessions are held in the casino areas, too. Reno residents and visitors love this rollicking music, one of America's most original art forms. The festival also features a New Orleans-style jazz brunch.

JULY. 2 days

National Basque Festival

Elko, Nevada

Admission charged
Contact: Bob Echeverria, 1101 Court St., Elko, NV 89801

Basques living in the western states trace their origins to the Pyrenees, between Spain and France. Emigration to this country began at the turn of the century, and many of the new arrivals took up sheepherding. The lonely, nomadic life of a shepherd encouraged individuality and tremendous physical strength. This strength is very much a part of the Basque tradition today, and is annually demonstrated at this celebration.

Events include lifting a 250-lb cylinder as many times as possible, hefting a 225-lb granite ball to the shoulder where it is rolled around the neck, even a brisk walk is complicated by 107-lb weights in each hand. These are not the only measures of endurance at the festival: logs with a diameter of 54' have to be quickly chopped in half, massive concrete weights are dragged 120-feet, and carefully spaced beer cans have to be collected one at a time and then run to a trash can. The traditional climax of all these games is a stupendous tug-of-war between warring teams from different cities. Tremendous amounts of food must be eaten to keep up with this outpouring of energy, and the Basque feast is more than a match for the appetites built up by the competitions. On Saturday a parade enlivens the business district of Elko, with floats, musicians and traditional dancers with their intricate steps. Perhaps the most unique contest in a weekend devoted to unusual accomplishments is the *irrinitzi* contest. The *irrinitzi* is a loud, wavering war cry launched from the Basque people's past, and each year it echoes eerily throughout Elko's city park.

EARLY AUGUST. 1 weekend

Gift of the Waters

Thermopolis, Wyoming

Free
Contact: Chamber of Commerce, State Park Bldg., Thermopolis, WY 82443

In 1896, the Shoshone and Arapahoe tribes sold the world's largest mineral hot springs to the people of Wyoming. The Indians received $60,000 for the

Tepee Fountain, a colorful formation of mineral water deposits.

springs and ten surrounding acres. Chief Washakie requested that a portion of the waters remain free to the public. In accordance with his wish, one-fourth of the waters from the springs has been set aside for free use. The Shoshones referred to the springs as *Bah-gue-wana*, which means 'Smoking Waters' in their language. This transaction is celebrated each year at Hot Springs State Park in a pageant written in tribute to Chief Washakie. Other activities include shoot-outs in downtown Thermopolis, the traditional Saturday morning parade, zany melodrama performances in the evenings, a free buffalo tasting and a demolition derby. Shoshones from the reservation camp in tepees near the Big Spring. The area offers good trout and walleye fishing, as well as spectacular hiking along canyon trails through the geologic history of Wyoming.

A community celebration drawing artists from the entire West, this weekend event takes you through the full range of arts and crafts in this wild and remote corner of America. Located on the North Idaho College campus, the festival also features a variety of home-cooked food for sale and a Clothesline Sale with works priced under $25. You'll enjoy the juried art show and a booth offering direct sales from artists to the public. Children are entertained in a special section where clay, paint, paper and supervision are provided to budding artists. A joyful series of performing events continue into the evenings, including music, dance, theatre, puppetry and clowns. Music ranges from classical to folk, bluegrass and jazz. Friday evening is theatre night and Saturday is ballet.

EARLY AUGUST. 3 days

Art on the Green

Coeur d'Alene, Idaho

Free
Contact: Citizens Council for the Arts, Box 901, Coeur d'Alene, ID 83814

AUGUST. 2 days

Park City Art Festival

Park City, Utah

Admission charged
Contact: Kimball Art Center, P.O. Box 1880, Park City, UT 84060

A tiny town, only a few blocks long, hidden in the mountains of Utah, with a population of over 100,000?

Sounds astounding, yet that's Park City during the annual art fair. What bedlam! Don't even think about driving on Main Street. Between the exhibitors and the spectators, you'll be lucky to walk the few blocks in under an hour. But what a time you'll have, and what art you'll see. All kinds of art are for sale here—painting, drawing, photography, printmaking, clay, glass, fiber, leather, jewelry, metal, wood, and stone. Everything is eligible, so long as the work is original. Over 200 artists show here. In addition to the visual arts, the visitor can watch mime troupes, eat good food ranging from hot dogs to exotic ethnic cuisine, and listen to all kinds of music. Concerts include classical, country & western, reggae, blue grass, jazz, swing and good old rock'n roll.

AUGUST. 9 days

Festival of Nations

Red Lodge, Montana

Free
Contact: Chamber of Commerce, P.O. Box 998, Red Lodge,
MT 59068

Friendly Montanans reached out helping hands to neighbors during the frontier era, and this spirit of pioneer hospitality is celebrated annually in the Festival of Nations. Eight European nationalities homesteaded and settled here in the 1800s and each are represented with a day and evening of festive events. The Germans, Scandinavians, Finns, Italians, Yugoslavs, English-Irish and Scots each stage special events celebrating their heritage.

During the day, hungry visitors trek to the International Cooking Pavilion for free samples of ethnic specialities, with different selections each day. In the evenings each nationality performs at the Civic Center with costumed singers, traditional bands, intricate European Folk dances, pageants, plays and skits. The festival culminates with an All Nations Day symbolizing the ethnic amalgam of America. Local arts and crafts are shown all week, and the schools hold special exhibits. The entire population of Red Lodge is less than 2,000 people, but each year they entertain more than twenty-five times their own numbers in a gala celebration of Montana spirit.

❋ *AUTUMN* ❋

LABOR DAY WEEKEND. 3 days

Wagon Days

Ketchum, Idaho

Most events free
Contact: Chamber of Commerce, P.O. Box 2420, Sun Valley,
ID 83353

The town of Ketchum remembers its past as a mining community when the West was wild and wooly. Each year a big parade is the centerpiece of this celebration. No motorized vehicles are allowed and over 100 entries march downtown including bands, drill teams and beauty queens. The highlights of the whole parade are six enormous, antique ore wagons drawn by straining horses. Originally used in the last century to carry ore from the high country, these wagons are the traditional heart of the parade. A Flapjack Breakfast is held on both Saturday and Sunday mornings, drawing hundreds of hungry celebrants. Several premier bicycle races are run including a criterium, road race and time trials. Antique and peddler fairs are set up to sell all sorts of art, furniture, quilts, dolls, jewelry and other collectables. Ketchum's most famous citizen is commemorated each year in the play *E. Hemingway* performed every night at the Old City Hall. The outdoor ice rink hosts an evening buffet and special Ice Show. Various barbecues and musical performances take place throughout the weekend, and a regional Chili Cook-Off is held on Sunday.

SEPTEMBER. 2 days

International Whistle-Off

Carson City, Nevada

Free
Contact: International Whistle-Off, 1191 S. Carson St.,
Carson City, NV 89701

"**W**ithout aid of a musical contrivance in the jowls or under the tongue," entrants in the Whistle-Off try to whistle their way to glory. Fortunately, however, whistlers are allowed to use their hands or fingers to aid in their musical interpretations.

Contest categories include performances of classical or contemporary music, a dual competition for pairs and a curious category for so-called Novelty Whistling. The Whistle-Off has attracted contestants from around the country, and some from as far away as Canada, Australia and England. Spectators enjoy the contestants and are further entertained by guest performers, including a whistler/singer from Mexico and a Swedish naturalist famous for his musical whistling as well as his imitation bird calls. Some whistlers perform music, others accompany recorded or live music with interesting arpeggios and trills not normally heard from human lips.

Ingenuity in constructing booths is rewarded with prizes at most chili cookoffs. This one, by Dennis Mabry of Shingle Springs, CA, has won many awards, as has his chili.

SEPTEMBER. 3 days

Great High Sierra Chili Cook-Off

Carson City, Nevada

Entry fee charged to contestants
Contact: Bill Ruff Productions, 1817 Alpine St., Carson City,
NV 89701

What contains, among other ingredients, a fried field mouse, hot chicken lips, road apples, TNT powder, tequilla (with worm) and cigar ashes? It can only be High Sierra chili. This regional cook-off of the International Chili Society has fielded top prize-winning cooks in the World Championship. Entrants from all round the country compete here.

Watching chili simmer on the stove is supposedly about as interesting as watching paint dry, so the cooks dress up their booths with fantastic and outlandish details. Most have an Old West look to them, loosely interpreted by the kind of minds that

Allison and Dean Taylor, with son Jonathan, accept the $500 cash prize, trophy and other goodies for winning the 7th Annual Great High Sierra Chili Cookoff from event chairman, Bill Ruff, left. Their 'Taylor Made Chili' took second place at the 1984 World's Championship Chili Cookoff, missing the win by only one point!

claim dog food as the secret ingredient in their special chili recipe. Most cooks are costumed and some sing, tell stories, play music and generally act their way through the business of making chili. Judges aren't allowed to compare notes, choke, gasp or fall on the floor during tastings and they are usually well supplied with beer to cleanse their palates between bites. Cash prizes and trophies are awarded. The winners advance to the World Championship finals.

OCTOBER. 2 weekends

Harvest Festival

Monte Vista, Colorado

Admission charged
Contact: Chamber of Commerce, Monte Vista, CO 81144

The picturesque San Luis Valley of Colorado is loaded with rich farmland ideal for grain and potatoes. In the fall, Monte Vista holds a Harvest Festival to celebrate the talents of the local folks. The first weekend opens with an evening of local musicians performing classical music. A public reception follows. The next night brings an art show highlighting local artists. Art in the Park is an arts and crafts show with plenty of entertainment and food booths. The community produces a favorite musical to wrap up the second weekend and each year wins bigger praise.

Pacific Coast

Bishop Homecoming Rodeo.

Festival of the Arts, Laguna Beach.

Cinco de Mayo Parade in San Jose.

Tournament of Roses Queen and Royal Court.

The Monterey Jazz Festival.

NOVEMBER OR DECEMBER. 1 day

Doo Dah Parade

Pasadena, California

Free
Contact: Doo Dah Parade, 78 N. Marengo, Rm. 26, Pasadena, CA 91101

Born as an alternative to Pasadena's world-famous Rose Parade, the Doo Dah Parade is everything most parades aren't: irreverent, disorganized, zany and off-the-wall. Possessing no theme, judges, prizes, order or motorized vehicles, the Doo Dah still manages to stage a day of hilarity for tens of thousands of spectators.

Parade entries vary each year but have included such luminaries as the Attachables, a marching group executing precision choreography featuring Velcro. The Dull Men's Club of Newport Beach boringly tromps the parade route. One cheapskate refuses to cover her float (a large beat-up skate) with rose petals for the other parade and makes do with paper mache and the Doo Dah. The Budsdale Clydeweisers features horses pulled by a six-pack of beer. Two L.A. waitresses dressed as bag ladies carry signs proclaiming "I'm not a waitress, I'm an actress!" The Olympic gold medal hula hoop team spirals down the road. The Amazon River Swim Team shows up with shredded swimsuits, piranha fish still attached. Spirited music is provided by the Garbage Can Drum Corps. Where else could you see Mutant Queens, Nerdbusters and the infamous Santa Monica Broke Dancers? One group, the Synchronized Briefcase Drill Team, has rocketed to stardom (of sorts) since their appearance in the first Doo Dah Parade. Begun as a group of well-regimented investment bankers, they are now a non-profit organization with their own pinstriped stationery. The wonder of it all is how the Doo Dah organizers manage year after year to convince the city fathers to close the streets for this unique brand of parade zaniness.

Rose Parade

Pasadena, California

Free
Contact: Tournament of Roses Association, 391 S. Orange
Grove Blvd., Pasadena, CA 91105

Millions upon millions of flower petals and blossoms, plus tons of leaves, seeds, grass, spices and moss annually travel the 5½-mile march of the Rose Parade. Enormous floats, some fifty feet long, are constructed and each exposed part must be covered with vegetation and natural materials. Most floats carry riders who salute and wave to parade watchers, and many are animated with moving characters. Though not the oldest parade in the country, nonetheless the Rose Parade receives the widest viewership. Over a million spectators see it from the curbs and stands in Pasadena, and another 125 million watch its televised presentations, some sent by satellite to Europe and Japan. A few past entries have included a huge camel constructed of sun-bleached moss dusted with cinnamon; an old-fashioned sternwheeler showboat adorned with white mums, roses, orchids, iris and other flowers; two enormous striped tigers of chrysanthemums, calendulas and marigolds; and the entire cityscape of downtown Los Angeles reproduced in flowers. The floats aren't the only entrants in the parade; 22 bands are also invited and over 200 equestrians ride their horses along Colorado Boulevard.

Sponsored by a non-proft organization of volunteers, the Rose Parade has been held since 1890, and has only very rarely been rained upon. On New Year's afternoon and all day January 2nd, the floats can be viewed up close as they are parked along Sierra Madre Boulevard. After the parade, the great granddaddy of all bowl games is played with a football team representing the Pac-10 vying with a team from the Big Ten.

Winter Carnival

Sierra Ski Ranch, Twin Bridges, California

No entry fee or lift ticket charge for any contest
Contact: Sierra Ski Ranch, P.O. Box 3501, Twin Bridges, CA
95735

South of Lake Tahoe, one spiny ridge of national forest has been groomed for skiers. Snowy trails and

nine chairlifts rise above a ski ranch. Each winter skiing enthusiasts race and cavort in a four-day carnival. Daily costume contests are held with prizes for the most imaginative. Many special skiing events take place, including professional races, a handicapped skiers event, a senior citizens race, youth and children's events, a Snowshoe Thompson Historical Ski race and the barrel staves race. Other celebrants can compete in a snow sculpture contest, a snowshoe cocktail foot race, a chili cook-off or an ice cream eating contest. Every evening sees a gala apres-ski party and the awarding of daily prizes.

FEBRUARY TO OCTOBER. 6 months

Oregon Shakespearean Festival

Ashland, Oregon

Admission charged
Contact: Oregon Shakespearean Festival, P.O. Box 158,
Ashland, OR 97520

A major cultural resource in the West, the Oregon Shakespearean Festival in Ashland is entering its

The outdoor Elizabethan Stage of the Oregon Shakespearean Festival, Ashland.

sixth decade. It has grown from a modest endeavor in 1935 whose success surprised everyone, to a Tony-winning regional theatre. During the season, twelve plays are presented in three theatres—the Elizabethan Stage, the Black Swan and the new Angus Bowmer Theatre named for the festival founder. Besides Shakespeare, outstanding classic and contemporary plays are also showcased. The festival offers backstage tours, workshops, classes and lectures as well as an Exhibit Center where visitors can try on costumes and strut on the stage.

In the coming years, productions will range from the sunny comedy *As You Like It*, to the magical *Tempest*, and the savage blood-letting of *Titus Andronicus*. Shakespeare wrote the whole range of human experience onto his Renaissance stage. Each year these majestic plays are performed in Oregon for devoted audiences numbering in the hundreds of thousands.

JANUARY/FEBRUARY. 2 weekends

Alpenfest

Mt. Shasta, California

Free
Contact: Chamber of Commerce, 300 Pine St., Mount Shasta,
CA 96067

The whole family enjoys the varied attractions of Alpenfest. The first weekend features dog sled races as teams from all over the nation compete in various events. The next weekend opens with an ice scupture contest as chilly works of art are erected around the city. The children love the Teddy Bear Parade where they can dress up as their favorite bear. Sportsmen can enter the Nordic Slalom or Cross-Country Ski Races. Local merchants compete in a Cross-Country Relay for the Perpetual Trophy. Snowmobiles are judged in six different categories, and local dealers hold a snowmobile show. If there is enough snow, visitors can sit back and enjoy horse-drawn sleigh rides around the city; if the weather is balmy, wagon rides are offered. A King and Queen are crowned. The noisiest event, a Yodel-Off Contest is held with competitors coming from all around the country to demonstrate their loudest, and most authentic, Alpine yodels.

FEBRUARY/MARCH. 3 days

Almond Blossom Festival

Ripon, California

Free
*Contact: Chamber of Commerce, P.O. Box 327, Ripon, CA
        96366*

Surprisingly, the almond is California's largest tree crop. Not so surprising, though, is Ripon's desire to

celebrate this bountiful crop with a beautiful spring festival. Held when the almond trees are blossoming, this hometown festival includes tours of the orchards and the almond processing plant. A needlework and baked goods sale, hobby show, art show and antique display also beckon. A local winery holds tours and tastings. A mouthwatering almond bake-off and auction will tempt the gourmands. Miss Almond Blossom is crowned and rides in the grand parade downtown. Both a tractor pull and a tractor rodeo are held. Good food is plentiful at the smorgasbord, ham breakfast and chicken barbecues. Dances include one for teens, a family dance and a Swiss festival dance. A carnival plays all three days with exhibits and displays at the community center.

❋ SPRING ❋

MID-MARCH. 2 days each

Whale Festivals

Mendocino and Fort Bragg, California

Admission charged to some events
*Contact: Chamber of Commerce, P.O. Box 1141, Fort Bragg,
        CA 95437*

California gray whales need warm waters to give birth to their calves. Annually they migrate from cold northern waters to the lagoons of Baja where the babies are born. In the late winter and early spring they begin their return trip up the coast, and mid-March is the best time to catch sight of them. The grays stay fairly close to the coast, perhaps navigating by sight. During this time of year a series of Whale Festivals are held with special whale-watching tours and cruises. Other events include wine tastings, art shows, home tours, a 10k run and clam chowder cookoff.

APRIL, 1 day

Crabfeed & Auction

Bainbridge Island, Washington

Admission charged
Contact: Bainbridge Arts & Crafts, Inc., 155 Winslow Way
East, Bainbridge Island, WA 98110

A community effort to support the arts in Bainbridge Island, the annual Crabfeed and Auction is an annual success. Tickets go on sale a couple weeks ahead of the event and sell out quickly. Participants are treated to a generous dinner of crab, salad, French bread, dessert and wine. The auction raises money for scholarships and arts programs in the schools. Items sold include baskets of chocolates, evenings at local restaurants, tickets to the Seattle Sonics games, a dinner cruise on a luxurious boat and a week in a Hawaiian condo. Art objects by guild members are also auctioned.

APRIL, 4 days

Apple Blossom Festival

Sebastopol, California

Most events free
Contact: Chamber of Commerce, P.O. Box 178, Sebastopol,
CA 95472

O ver 8,000 acres of orchards carpet the hillsides around Sebastopol, many of them planted with Gravensteins. The Gravenstein is a unique apple, first planted in this area by the Russians at Fort Ross and now a major part of the local economy. In spring, the orchards are in full bloom setting the stage for this local celebration. Contests abound, a Queen is crowned in an elaborate coronation show, then a parade moves down Main Street to the tunes of a Dixieland jazz band.

An art show and a crafts fair are both set up. Runners compete in 10k and two-mile Apple Juice Runs. Everyone enjoys the free band concerts in the park where pancakes are sold at breakfast time and chicken is barbecued all afternoon. Teenagers and square dancers each have their own dance. A bright wildflower show is featured. And, surrounding the city are the reasons for it all, the abundant apple blossoms. Apple ranches hold tours all weekend. The visitor probably won't be able to tell the Gravenstein tree from the Rome Beauty, or the Red Delicious from the Golden, but the trees are all beauties at this time of year.

APRIL, 3 days

International Teddy Bear Convention

Nevada City, California

Admission charged
Contact: Pat Coberl, Curator, American Victorian Museum,
Nevada City, CA 95959

Although Teddy Bears are usually thought of as children's playthings, this convention conclusively proves otherwise. Teddies from all over the world, manufactured or handmade, of every size, shape and description meet here annually to strut their stuff and look for new homes. Owners display their collections for show and dealers sell Teddies and bear paraphernalia. Other dolls are seasonal, but Teddies are forever.

Ever since Theodore Roosevelt refused to shoot a black bear on a hunting expedition, bear dolls named for him have curled up to sleep next to little children. Since most of us have owned a teddy at one time or another, and most of them aren't thrown away but make their way to garage sales and swap meets, there may be more teddies in the United States than people. No wonder they have their own convention.

APRIL, 2 weeks

San Francisco International Film Festival

San Francisco, California

Admission charged
Contact: San Francisco International Film Festival, 3501 California St., Suite 201, San Francisco, CA 94118

Cinema fans sit in darkened San Francisco theaters and view the best in international film—new films from all over the world, retrospectives of the best from the past and tributes to influential filmmakers and stars. The San Francisco Film Festival is a celebration of film as an art form. The oldest event of its kind in the United States, this two-week festival's main program is non-competitive. Features and shorts of unusually high quality are screened daily. Recent festival-goers enjoyed a French film spoofing a decadent cabaret, a British movie about a runaway teenager, a New York film depicting Forty-Second Street's world of junkies, a moody Swedish movie of love and murder, a Czech film on an unexpected village marriage and dozens more. The festival also sponsors a competition for 16mm films, videos and TV specials. Outstanding entries in these categories are also screened for the public.

LATE APRIL, 10 days

Los Angeles Bach Festival

Los Angeles, California

Admission charged
Contact: Los Angeles Bach Festival, First Congregational Church of Los Angeles, 540 S. Commonwealth Ave., Los Angeles, CA 90020

Over two hundred years after his death, this master of the baroque compositional form continues to inspire music lovers. The great bulk of Johann Sebastian Bach's work was composed for performance in the church, and the Los Angeles Bach Festival continues that tradition. Sponsored by and performed at the First Congregational Church, the Bach Festival brings guest artists of renown from all over the world. The Los Angeles Chamber Orchestra is the resident ensemble and singers from the church form the core

of the festival chorus. Concerts are held at noon and in the evenings. The noon concerts frequently feature young talent. For half a century, the Gothic-style Congregational Church has been bringing the music of Bach to Los Angeles in an appropriate, medieval, European-style setting.

The Sunnyvale Fremont High School marching band swings down Market Street in the Plaza Park area as it nears the reviewing stand. Their casual attire and excellent musicianship drew loud and appreciative applause from the over 50,000 people assembled to view the 148-unit parade.

MAY 5TH. 1 day

Cinco de Mayo

San Jose, California

Free
Contact: San Jose GI Forum, 1680 E. Santa Clara St., San Jose, CA 95116

On May 5, 1862, Mexican forces won an important victory against Napoleon III's army in Puebla, Mexico. This defeat of the French led eventually to Mexican independence and is celebrated every year on Cinco de Mayo. The San Jose GI Forum sponsors a huge parade and Fiesta to commemorate the victory, apparently the largest Cinco de Mayo celebration in the United States. The parade is viewed by nearly 100,000 celebrants. The large parade features Chicano entertainers from California as well as frequent appearances of Mexican headliners, decorated floats, marching bands, beauty queens and low rider cars. The Fiesta includes food and beer booths, entertainment and dancing. Performers vary each year, but San Jose has been able in past years to attract such famous groups as Luis Valdez' Teatro Campesino, *comida Mexicana* groups, top Chicano bands and Mexican *folklorico* dancers. Of course, *mariachi* bands play continuously.

Irrigation Festival

Sequim, Washington

Most events free
Contact: Chamber of Commerce, Box 907, Sequim, WA 98382

Lying in the rain shadow of the Olympic Mountains on the northern coast of the Olympic Peninsula, Sequim enjoys almost perpetual sunshine and meager rainfall. It was a barren valley until 90 years ago when a hearty crew dug an irrigation ditch from the Dungeness River and seemingly made water flow uphill to bring new life to the land.

This nine-day celebration, oldest in the state of Washington, includes the crowning of the festival Queen and her Princesses, a pageant, two parades, natural history exhibits, arts and crafts shows, special barbecues, a horse show, a demolition derby and horse shoe pitching.

THIRD WEEKEND IN MAY. 3 days

Jumping Frog Jubilee

Angels Camp, California

Admission charged
Contact: Chamber of Commerce, P.O. Box 177, San Andreas, CA 95249

Mark Twain transformed American folklore into literature when he wrote *The Celebrated Jumping Frog of Calaveras County.* Now residents of Angels Camp are keeping Twain's story alive every year with their Jubilee. Staged along with the county fair, the Jubilee annually pits athletic frogs against each other to see who can jump the farthest, vying against the world record of over twenty feet. Kids and seniors have special jumps, and heats are held throughout the whole weekend until the winning frog is found. Winners are awarded cash prizes, and $1500 is reserved for the champ who sets a new world's record. Contest entrants don't even need to own a frog since the Jubilee organizers offer a 'Rent-a-Frog' program for frogless enthusiasts. You can also hire a jockey to handle the frog if you lack the skills.

The Calaveras County Fair runs simultaneously with featured livestock exhibits and judgings, a Queen contest, kid's programs, dances, fireworks and a two-day professional rodeo. Frog jumping originated in the mining camps and '49ers would wager gold dust on the leaping abilities of their favorite frog. Miners' traditions and humor are kept alive each year in Angels Camp when the frogs start hopping again.

Mule Days

Bishop, California

Admission charged
Contact: Bishop Chamber of Commerce, 690 N. Main St.,
Bishop CA 93514

With a population of a thousand pesky mules, Bishop reigns as the 'Mule Capital of the World.' Each year the citizens fittingly celebrate these noble animals during Mule Days. The highlights of the festival are the mule shows held on each day of the weekend, where mules compete in races, steer roping,

packing contests and other events. Mule Days also offers an all-mule parade with beautiful pack strings, pleasure animals and crowd-pleasing comedy entries. A mule-shoeing contest is held. You can attend a dance, or a unique braying contest where mule people compete to see who can sound most like their animals.

MAY/JUNE (So. California)
AUGUST/SEPTEMBER (No. California). 6 weekends each

Renaissance Pleasure Faires

Agoura and Novato, California

Admission charged
Contact: The Blaine Group, 7465 Beverly Blvd., Los Angeles,
CA 90036

Hot buns from Banbury Cross are just one of the taste-tempting treats waiting to satisfy visitors to the annual Renaissance Pleasure Faire. International food favorites abound as the Faire adds such exotic dishes as piroshki, falafel, tempura, sushi, and trifle to its traditional favorites.

Each year Britain's Good Queen Bess brings her court to California for two giant festivals, in the south in spring and in the north during fall. Attended by her courtiers and suitors, the Queen reigns over six weekends of pageantry, theatre, crafts, music and dance. Authentically costumed shire folk join various guilds. St. Stephen's Guild consists of nobility, they lounge around the glen and discuss manners and fashions. St. Minerva's Guild members are lower-class women who spend the day gossiping around the local washing well. St Patrick's Guild is a group of bards passing through the shire singing and performing their music. Exhibition games and tournaments are played, including such sports as Foote Balle, Wench Lifting, Tug-of-War, Archery, Bandy Ball, Fencing and Haytoss. Masques, plays and comedias will be presented. Kissing, courtship and other social games of the mid-1500s will be taught to willing faire-goers.

A juried craft show is mounted, and many craftspeople will have booths selling and demonstrating their arts. Dances include rounds, rondelays, courtly quadrilles and peasant dances. Authentic food is sold throughout the day and night. Among the many celebrants, Sir Francis Drake, William Shakespeare and Sir Walter Raleigh can be found every day.

The Grand Tournament of Horses is one of the most colorful and enjoyed events of the Renaissance Pleasure Faire.

JUNE. 5 days

Flower Festival

Lompoc, California

Most events free
*Contact: Lompoc Valley Festival Assoc., 113-C North I St.,
Lompoc, CA 93438*

Two thousand acres are carpeted in sweet peas, nasturtiums, marigolds, petunias, zinnias, larkspur, delphinium, poppies, stock and sweet alyssum in a crazy quilt of blooming colors. Lompoc is an east-west running valley near the coast. It has a mild climate with ample moisture from rain and fog, and soil rich with alluvial deposits. Since the turn of the century, horticulturalists have experimented with growing flower seeds here. Now several large firms, and many individual family farms, produce millions of flower seeds sold around the world.

In June the fields are reaching full bloom, and Lompoc celebrates with an annual Flower Festival. A big parade winds through town with marching bands, drill teams, clowns, equestrians and floats decorated all in flowers. A carnival is set up, and Ryon Park features 34 different food booths, free entertinment, commercial exhibits and sales. A big fireworks display lights the skies on opening night. Guided bus tours of the fields depart all day on Saturday and Sunday, and motorists will find maps available for self-guided tours. A huge flower show highlights the festival with displays by local arrangers, garden clubs and growers.

Nearby Mission La Purisima celebrates the Flower Festival, too. Here visitors step back to the early 1800s to view a working mission with docents demonstrating the daily life of Padres and Indians.

Myth California Pageant

San Diego, California

Free
Contact: Cross Your Heart Support Network, San Diego, CA

Wacky demonstrations highlight the week of this feminist anti-festival. A take-off on the Miss California Pageant, Myth California supporters drive floats around town on no set course. One year a public vomiting was staged, to dramatize the plight of those women afflicted with eating disorders and to protest the sponsors of the Miss California Pageant (it was

their products that were vomited). Themes of the pageant have included 'No More Profits from Women's Bodies,' 'Endorsing Women as Sex Objects Endorses Rape,' 'Judge Meat Not Women,' and 'Weight Slavery.' This Pageant is the brainchild of artist Nikki Craft and dramatically showcases many popular feminist themes.

Summer Solstice Parade

Santa Barbara, California

Free
Contact: Chamber of Commerce, 1330 State St., Santa Barbara, CA 93101

Block-long dragons of colorful helium balloons snake above the heads of parade-watchers as the Solstice Parade marches up State Street. Originated by a group of local artists, this event has become one of the most original and spectacular parades in the country. Participants aren't allowed to ride in motorized vehicles or to carry signs. Huge paper mache puppets manipulated by six or seven costumed marchers bob and weave down the streets. Belly dancers undulate to the tunes of Arabic instruments, a drum corps annually announces its presence with tremendous percussions. Many entries are clever visual puns, several act out little skits in each block. Costumed ants fiercely chase

a paper mache picnic, intent on devouring the last bite. Bogus policewomen ticket the viewers lining the street for having too much fun. After the parade a huge concert is held in a local park with parade entrants and watchers mingling together. The end of the parade and the beginning of the concert is usually heralded by a mass release of tens of thousands of balloons that literally fill the sky.

MID-JULY THROUGH AUGUST, 6 weeks

Festival of Arts

Laguna Beach, California

Admission charged
Contact: Festival of Arts, 650 Laguna Canyon Rd., Laguna Beach, CA 92651

Residents of Laguna Beach, often called Lagunatics, stage an enormous art festival every summer. The largest event of its kind in the West, it features hundreds of artists displaying a wide range of media—paintings, etchings, drawings, serigraphs, photography, stained glass, weavings, wood carvings, jewelry, ceramics, furniture and model making. All exhibits are for sale, and the celebration attracts visitors from all over the country. Festival grounds are carpeted with sweeping lawns, spacious picnic areas, and house two restaurants. Plenty of events are planned for children including a student art show, junior art workshops with free materials and instruction and daily puppet shows. Sundays bring ballet performances, and various other musical programs are put on throughout the six-week period.

This festival's central attraction is the nightly performance of the Pageant of Masters. Using real people posing in costumes against authentically reproduced backgrounds, the Pageant of Masters re-creates art of the great masters. These living pictures take much skill to reproduce, and provide an excursion through the great art of the world. With careful lighting, costumes and backgrounds the live performers take on the appearance of a real painting or live sculpture, deceiving the eyes of festival-goers. The festival is successful enough to provide thousands of scholarship dollars to local art students and organizations.

The original of this exquisite gold lacquer Oriental pill box with inlay of mother of pearl, ivory, and coral is only a few inches high. This Pageant of the Masters reproduction stands 11 feet tall on the Irvine Bowl stage to accomodate the live models.

leather goods, paintings as well as garlic graphics on t-shirts, hats and books. This savory festival began in 1979, inspired by reports of a tiny French town that drew thousands to its yearly garlic fete. In five years the Gilroy Garlic Festival's attendance has grown from 20,000 to 120,000.

One major festival highlight is the Great Garlic Recipe Contest and Cook Off. Ten top finalists, chosen from the hundreds who submit original garlic recipes, face off before a panel of nationally known food critics in the kitchen of nearby Gilroy High School. Entertainment is continuous from four different stages featuring mariachis, the Garlic Queen Contest (crowned with a garlic bulb tiara), puppeteers, mimes, clowns and garlic braiding contests. You can also participate in bike tours, golf and tennis tournaments, and a 10k Great Garlic Gallop.

JULY. 3 days

Gilroy Garlic Festival

Gilroy, California

Admission charged
Contact: Garlic Festival, Box 2311, Gilroy, CA 95020

Will Rogers described Gilroy as "The only town in America where you can marinate a steak by hanging it on the clothesline." The Garlic Capital of the World promises to dazzle you with its culinary wizards— tossing spectacular skillets of flaming calamari, grilling mountains of garlic bread and stir-frying bushels of vegetables fresh from fields in full view. Talented amateur chefs of Gourmet Alley perform to benefit their chosen charities, sauteeing scampi in lobster butter sauce, stuffing giant mushrooms and basting huge slabs of sirloin with rosemary mops dunked in garlic marinade. Wines from the Santa Clara Valley complement the convivial meals.

While nibbling on garlicky appetizers or enjoying a movable feast, festival-goers may browse through the open-air marketplace for garlic in all its guises: fresh, braided, pills, books of legend and mystery, and even 14K gold garlic may be found. Nearly 200 booths in the open air marketplace, feature both garlic and regional arts and crafts including pottery, metal work,

MID-JULY THROUGH AUGUST. 6 weeks

Britt Music Festival

Jacksonville, Oregon

Admission charged
Contact: Peter Britt Gardens Music and Arts Festival
Association, P.O. Box 1124, Medford, OR 97501

Rich orchestral sounds bathe the hillside near the quaint Gold Rush village of Jacksonville, Oregon. Each year thousands of music lovers attend the varied concerts of the Britt Music Festival, now over twenty years old. One of the most enchanting summer music festivals, the Britt is still intimate enough that parking is easy, tickets are plentiful and the concerts are not mobbed. Actually four diffferent festivals in one, the visitor can enjoy jazz, bluegrass, dance or classical presentations. Each year music director John Trudeau assembles a classical orchestra from members of various western symphonies and books a wide variety of outstanding soloists. At the Britt concerts the weather is usually wonderful, the acoustics in the new wooden pavilion are superb and the audience enjoys the music from a hillside overlooking the scenic Rogue River Valley.

AUGUST. 3 days

Omak Stampede & Suicide Race

Omak, Washington

Admission charged
Contact: Omak Stampede, Box 916, Omak, WA 98841

Not for the squeamish, these Suicide Races are aptly named. A headlong rush on horseback down a steep dirt hillside, followed by a swim across 200 yards of swiftly moving river, a dash up the riverbank and a sprint into the rodeo arena—that's a race? And some racers and their mounts enter more than one run-

ning. These macho activities punctuate each of the four rodeo performances on this explosive weekend. More reflective souls can visit a traditional Indian village with costumed dancers, or attend the fun-filled carnival. Two parades march rather more sedately along the streets, one for children and one for adults, complete with the crowning of a regal Queen. More contemplative visitors can stroll slowly through a western art show.

AUGUST. 1 week

Steinbeck Festival

Salinas, California

Pre-registration required
Contact: Steinbeck Center, John Steinbeck Library, 110 W. San Luis St., Salinas, CA 93901

This festival brings together the world's leading authorities on Pulitzer- and Nobel-winning novelist John Steinbeck in order to promote a greater understanding and appreciation of Salinas' most famous citizen. Faculty and panelists include professors from all over the America, as well as Japan, Korea and India. In addition to the academics, participants include some old childhood friends and cronies of Steinbeck, including Sparky Enea, once a fisherman and cook aboard the *Sea of Cortez*. All Steinbeck fans owe it to themselves to visit 'Steinbeck Country,' see Cannery Row, Big Sur and the Salinas Valley. Events at the festival include lectures, seminars, plays and films, plus a walking tour of the author's hometown.

AUGUST. 5 days

Old Spanish Days

Santa Barbara, California

Most events free
Contact: Old Spanish Days, 1122 North Milpas St., Santa Barbara, CA 93103

The sun-drenched streets and red-tiled roofs of Santa Barbara resound all week to the cries of *Ole!*

Each year the gracious city celebrates its Spanish and Mexican heritage in a gala fiesta. Confetti showers down as *cascarones* (confetti-filled eggs) are smashed over the heads of parade watchers. A grand historical parade starts at the beach with a re-enactment of Juan Cabrillo's landing, then marches up State Street to Alameda Park. Bands, silver-saddled horses, historical floats, politicians in limousines, costumed Spanish ladies on spirited Arabian horses, Chumash Indians chanting and dancing, and mounted sheriff's posses. Friday brings *La Cabalgata,* a promenade of richly outfitted horses and carriages.

Saturday is *El Desfilo de los Ninos,* the children's parade. No motorized vehicles are allowed in this parade. The youngsters walk the parade route in charming and, often hilarious costumes. Neighborhood groups come dressed as Mexican dinners, complete with walking tacos; dogs, cats, and even hens wear sombreros; sleeping babies are pulled in wagons by toddlers wearing authentic costumes from Spain and Mexico; tiny vaqueros and Spanish dancers grace the street; and costumed flower girls toss blossoms to the crowd. A four-day rodeo plays at the Earl Warren Showgrounds, with competitions for local cowboys as well as professionals. Street parties and dancing take place every evening and a variety show is held in the sunken gardens of the monumental old courthouse. Fiesta markets around town dispense Mexican specialties. *Mariachi* music, Spanish dancing, children's art exhibits and theatrical presentations take place at La Casa de la Raza, the Chicano community center.

LABOR DAY WEEKEND. 3 days

Bishop Homecoming &
Labor Day Rodeo

Bishop, California

*Contact: Bishop Chamber of Commerce, 690 N. Main St.,
Bishop, CA 93514*

In the 1930s, Bishop suffered a dramatic exodus as Los Angeles displaced residents by buying up enormous tracts of land and water rights. Homecoming was started then to re-unite old friends and provide an occasion to share memories. Since then the festivities have grown and now include a full-blown rodeo. Like every homecoming, Bishop crowns a Queen, holds a dance and a parade. A favorite event is the Old-Timers Picnic where old friends and new acquaintances can get together. The rodeo features both professional competitors and local cowboys.

SEPTEMBER. 2 days

Danish Days

Solvang, California

*Most events free
Contact: Chamber of Commerce, Box 465, Solvang, CA 93463*

Solvang is an Old World Danish town in the heart of central California. A towering windmill beckons visitors, dozens of shops and restaurants offer imported Scandinavian goods. Belgian draft horses pull a Danish streetcar on a scenic tour.

Each September, the citizens celebrate their heritage with two days of Danish festivities. Puffy, round *aebleskivers* and *medisterpolse* sausage are sold at outdoor breakfasts. Musical groups, dancers and a children's chorus all perform, while Danish films are shown. Shakespeare's Hamlet about the tormented Danish prince is performed by local players. Roving bands of entertainers perform throughout the town, including a band atop the beer wagon, folk dancers and the spirited Solvang Singers. Most of the architecture in downtown Solvang is authentic Scandinavian, and during Danish Days citizens dress in costume giving you an Old World experience in the California hills.

SEPTEMBER. 3 days

Wooden Boat Festival

Port Townsend, Washington

Admission charged
Contact: Wooden Boat Foundation, 637 Water Street, Port Townsend, WA 98368

Interest in classically designed, hand-built wooden boats is growing fast, and the center of this revival is the Pacific Northwest. In the Victorian era, long before fiberglass speedboats, the cities lining Puget Sound each had a boathouse renting small, wooden rowing or sailing craft. Townspeople and tourists would rent a boat for an elegant outing on the calm waters of the Sound.

Today, these craft are again being built and collected, and several festivals are devoted to their promotion. The biggest and most comprehensive is the Wooden Boat Festival in tiny Port Townsend. Over 150 boats are displayed and workshops on boatbuilding, oar-making, sailmaking, planking, caulking and repairing are held. Both amateurs and professionals demonstrate their skills and the visitor can admire the graceful varnished planks of finished craft. Daily cruises are conducted, with dinner cruises in the evening. Saturday and Sunday both bring regattas, films and events for children.

Pendleton Round-Up

Pendleton, Oregon

Contact: The Pendleton Round-Up Assoc., P.O. Box 609, Pendleton, OR 97801

Billed as the fastest-moving rodeo in America, the Pendleton Round-Up is one of the biggest outdoor rodeos (and the second oldest) in the United States. Top cowboys compete in RCA-approved events, and local amateurs and riding clubs appear in such events as the wild cow milking, stagecoach races and wild horse races. Indians turn out in big numbers for this traditional western celebration. They gather at the campgrounds, perform traditional dances in costume, and take part in the colorful night pageant of *Happy Canyon*. A Queen of the American Indian Beauty Pageant is crowned with judging based on the beauty of the entrant's costume and horse trappings as well as her own beauty.

'Westward Ho!' is the theme of the Saturday parade depicting the history of transportation before the automobile. Authentically costumed cowboys and Indians join the parade on horseback, in mule wagons, Mormon coaches, logging carts, covered wagons and buggies. Each morning a Cowboy Breakfast is served in a local park, and Friday and Saturday nights a carnival, street dances, medicine shows and pony rides take over Main Street.

SEPTEMBER. 2 days

Street Scene Festival

Los Angeles, California

Free
Contact: General Services Department, City of Los Angeles

Only in Los Angeles could you find free entertainment from such stars as Joan Rivers, Richard Pryor, Stevie Wonder and Jackson Browne. Created in 1977 with the active backing of Mayor Tom Bradley, Street Scene is a huge, eclectic festival designed to bring people back into downtown Los Angeles. Attended by over a million people, this weekend offers a wide variety of entertainment. Twenty-one stages launch events as diverse as the many faces of Los Angeles itself. In music alone, there are over 300 live performances including rock'n roll, classical, jazz and ethnic groups. Where else could you watch the LA Rams cheerleaders, break dancers, a performance of the Square Dancers of America, the Ballet Espanol, the Aman Folk Ensemble and Joan Rivers all on the same day? Many shows are especially for children, and clowns stroll through the area. One hundred and fifty

arts and crafts booths offer goods from local artisans. Ethnic food booths sell many different specialties to hungry festival-goers. The celebration features a lively fireworks show Saturday night and a big parade on Sunday with marching bands, drill teams, equestrian units, folk dancers and floats.

THIRD WEEKEND IN SEPTEMBER. 3 days

Monterey Jazz Festival

Monterey, California

Admission charged, season tickets for arena available beginning April 1, grounds admission tickets available August 1.
Contact: Monterey Jazz Festival, P.O. Box JAZZ, Monterey, CA 93942

Grown weary of big city life in San Francisco, disc jockey Jimmy Lyons moved to the Monterey peninsula in the 1950s. Here he was able to realize his dream of a world-class jazz festival in a 'sylvan setting with lots of trees and grass and all that.' Each year the arena tickets sell out long before the event, as jazz fans anticipate hearing the best of jazz in the country's most beautiful setting. Five shows are held in the main arena, the Night Club is open from 8 p.m. to midnight each night of the festival, and Garden Stage shows run each afternoon. All the great names in jazz have played at Monterey, and many new talents have been introduced.

Johnny Appleseed Day

Paradise, California

Admission charged
Contact: Chamber of Commerce, 5800 Clark Rd., #3,
Paradise, CA 95969

The names alone are provocative—Delicious, Golden Delicious, Arkansas Black, Black Twig, Rome Beauty, Winesap, Winter Banana, McIntosh, Jonathan, Pippin, Maidenblush, Golden Rose and Granny Smith. Countless varieties of apples are grown in the high country around the small town of Paradise. Originally a mining area, Paradise Ridge is now mainly agricultural with the perfect climate for producing apples. Each year the citizens celebrate harvest with an all-day festival. The day opens with a hearty pancake breakfast under the pines. An apple pie social is held downtown with servings of pie topped with ice cream. A scenic run along the edge of Paradise Lake

will attract the athletic. The Park and Recreation Center hosts an arts and crafts show, club exhibits, commercial exhibits, movies, video games and continuous entertainment all day. Knowledgeable visitors flock to the Chamber of Commerce booth in the afternoon for the recipe contest bake sale. Throughout the day, all the local orchards welcome visitors to tour their facilities. When the whole family is finally tired of apples, they can retire to the Intermediate School for a giant spaghetti feed to finish the day.

Pumpkin Festival

Half Moon Bay, California

Free
Contact: Terry Pimsleur & Co., 2155 Union St., San Francisco,
CA 94123

Eager contestants from all over America, England and Canada enter candidates to the World Pumpkin Weigh-off. In 1984 the world champion squashed all records by weighing in at 612 pounds. At the tiny coastal town of Half Moon Bay more than 200,000 visitors come for the champion's parade and a slate of contests. The fog-shrouded hills turn bright orange in the fall while the telephone lines to Ohio, Nova Scotia and Sussex heat up as regional weights are called in.

Meanwhile, you can enter pie-eating contests, judge the multitude of pies that can come from one 500-pound giant, and browse through the adjoining fields to choose your family jack-o-lantern.

NOVEMBER/DECEMBER. 4 days

California Wine Festival

Monterey, California

Admission charged
Contact: California Wine Festival, P.O. Box WINE, Carmel,
CA 93921

Chardonnay, cabernet sauvignon, pinot noir, gewurztraminer, rose, blanc de noir, petite sirah, chenin blanc, sauvignon blanc, zinfandel, gamay beaujolais, pinot noir, merlot and champagne. All noble wines produced in the world's newest prestige winemaking country: California. The state's largest wine festival takes place each winter on the Monterey peninsula when winemakers and wine lovers get together to discuss their common passion. This lavish event attracts representatives from 100 California wineries, everyone from large manufacturers to small, family-operated wineries is on hand, representing all the winemaking regions of this large state.

Hundreds of wines are presented for sampling as winemakers from each company personally discuss the wines with festival-goers. Noted wine authorities, including big-name restaurateurs and chefs, conduct seminars. Gourmet meals are served in some of the peninsula's finest restaurants and country clubs. Ticket prices are high, but they enable the holder to attend the Grand Opening Reception, all seminars, the wine tastings every evening and five-course gourmet lunches.

Hawaii - Alaska - Canada

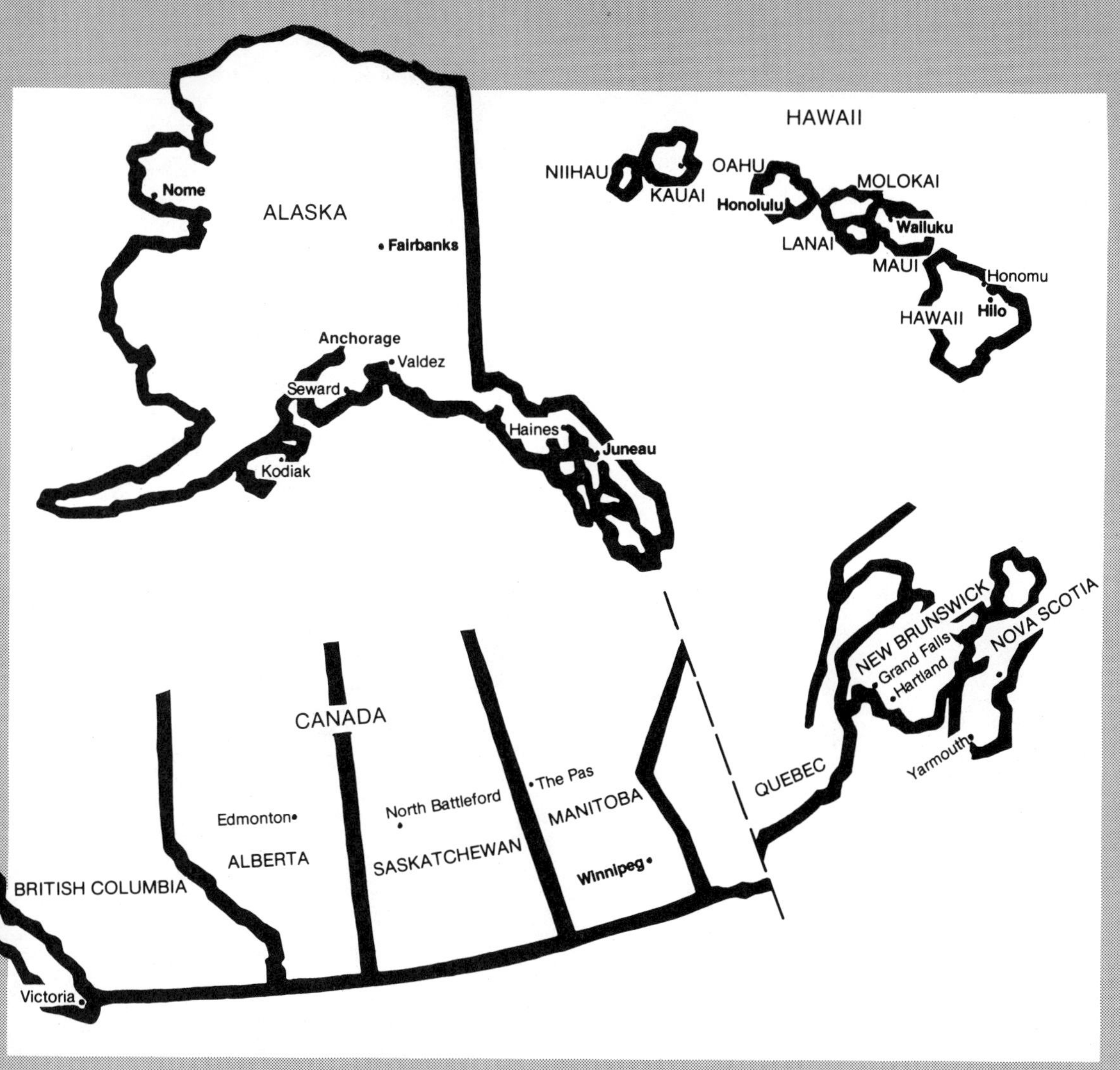

Folkfest entertainment in Victoria, British Columbia.

Celebrating Fairbanks' Golden Days.

Honolulu's Highland Gathering and Games.

Winter Carnival Skinny Ski Race, Valdez, Alaska.

MARCH. 1 day

Highland Gathering and Games

Honolulu, Hawaii

Admission charged
Contact: Stuart Cowan, Chieftain, 1600 Grosvenor Center,
733 Bishop St., Honolulu, HI 96813

Surprisingly, Scottish bagpipers march beneath towering palms in the balmy, tropic air of Hawaii. Sturdy Highlanders have established themselves even on this island paradise and are still keeping their own traditions alive. When James Cook reached Hawaii from England in 1778, two Scotsmen were among his crew. Ever since the Scots have participated in the life of the islands. They hold a special gathering every March at Richardson Field adjacent to the USS *Arizona* Memorial. Pipers and drummers from all around the Pacific attend, from Alaska to Australia. Dance and athletic competitions are held, including the kilted mile run, tug-of-war and hammer throw. Special clan tents help visitors trace their Scots ancestry. Stands sell Scottish food, clothing and crafts. And, somehow, at least on this one day of the year, it seems appropriate to see kilted clansmen marching in the equatorial sunshine.

MAY 1

Lei Day

Honolulu, Hawaii

Free
Contact: Hawaiana Section, Department of Parks and
Recreation, 650 South King St., Honolulu, HI 96813

In Hawaii, May Day is Lei Day as thousands of participants and viewers celebrate the fragrant, colorful beauty of this celebrated Hawaiian necklace. Adults and children both have a lei-making contest, and all entries are exhibited. A Lei Queen and her court are chosen, and traditional Hawaiian crafts are shown. In the evening, a Hula Pageant follows with dancing and entertainment. The following day, the leis are taken to the Royal Mausoleum and ceremonially presented to the ancient Hawaiian royalty.

Lei identifying committee.

Honomu Princess Float.

Honomu Village Fair

Honomu, Hawaii

Free
Contact: Fair Chairman, P.O. Box 186, Honomu, HI 96728

Honomu Village lies on the east coast of the island of Hawaii, in the shadow of Mauna Kea volcano. Like most island communities, it is a melting pot of Pacific cultures. Each summer residents stage a Village Fair, when the local population of 400 people swells to several thousand. Booths feature arts and crafts, baked goods and preserves, and white elephants looking for a new home. Sports include volleyball and softball tournaments, a greased pole climb and a beautiful seven-mile run to Akaka Falls. A parade is held on Saturday morning with clowns, bands, floats, marching groups, the roughriders and a Princess with her escorts. Children delight in the carnival and booths with special games. A variety of rides, games and contests are held, including the colorful Clown Costume Contest. Extroverts can enter the Lip Sync Contest judged by local disc jockeys. Everyone is remembered at this fair, even toddlers have a special Crawling Race. Delicious ethnic foods expressing the variety of the population are sold throughout the weekend.

Hula Festival

Honolulu, Hawaii

Free
*Contact: Hawaiiana Section, Department of Parks and
Recreation, 650 South King, Honolulu, HI 96813*

Sinuous and seductive, or fast-paced and energetic, the hula is one of Hawaii's most ancient art forms. Each August the Honolulu Department of Parks and Recreation keeps the traditional dances alive with a three-Sunday festival. The first Sunday is a large recital for all the students taking hula classes in the Parks and Recreation's summer classes. The following two Sunday performances are by invitation only, and involve private hula studios throughout the islands. Dancers in colorful muumuus and fresh flower leis perform both ancient and contemporary hulas. Everybody, from preschooler to senior citizen, sways to the rhythmic music of guitar and ukelele in this salute to the allure of native Hawaiian culture.

Aloha Week

Honolulu, Hawaii

Most events free
*Contact: Aloha Week Hawaii Inc., Suite 111, 750 Amana St.,
Honolulu, HI 96814*

Revelry and thanksgiving marked the ancient Hawaiian harvest festival. Held after crops were in and taxes paid, this week-long celebration honored the island royalty and the local gods as well as the bountiful gifts of the land. Aloha Week is the modern equivalent of this festival, started just after World War II as a conscious effort to preserve the ceremonies, dances, philosophy and music of Hawaii's past.

Aloha Week both opens and closes with an enormous street party. The first, in downtown Honolulu's financial district, offers a variety of entertainment and cuisine, including traditional Hawaiian, Chinese, Korean and even country & western. The second party is on Waikiki Beach where the major hotels open their public areas for visitors to stroll through and enjoy. Ten stages in this area present everything from hulas to military brass bands. During the week a variety of cultural events takes place. Each year's schedule is different, but special art exhibits, concerts and performances are presented, many featuring artists from as far away as Japan. Sporting events are held too, and this list is constantly changing and expanding. A central attraction this week is the beautiful Floral Parade with marching bands, floats and mounted units. The festival ends with a dramatic fireworks display the last evening.

· ALASKA ·

FEBRUARY. 10 days

Anchorage Fur Rendezvous

Anchorage, Alaska

Most events free

Contact: Fur Rendezvous, 737 W. 5th Avenue, Box 100773, Anchorage, AK 99510

It takes plenty of snow and ice, months of short winter days and multiple cases of cabin fever to generate enough pent-up energy for a really gigantic winter festival, all of which Anchorage has in quantity. Begun fifty years ago, the Fur Rendezvous has grown into an enormous celebration, affectionately called 'Rondy' by its participants. Many events are reminiscent of Alaska's heritage, notably the men's, women's and junior Championship Sled Dog Races and the Dog Weight-Pulling Contest. Long a major fur trapping area, Fur Rendezvous has always featured a Fur Auction with buyers from around the world bidding for wholesale furs. There is also a Fur Fashion Show with a champagne brunch. Native crafts are exhibited and demonstrated, and native dances are performed along with an Eskimo Blanket Toss. Frozen Illusions, a snow sculpture contest, is a fairly recent Rondy event that has even gained the attention of national television. A Queen is chosen and wears her royal furs in the Grand Parade. Over 4,000 festival-goers celebrate in costume at the Miner's and Trapper's Ball, with the best costumes winning prizes.

Downhill Canoe Race.

Many of Alaska's outdoor sports are practiced during Rondy, including cross country skiing, Nordic ski jumping, speedskating, curling, balloon racing and snowshoe racing. Other sports are parodied in a downhill canoe race across the frozen hills, snowshoe softball tournaments, snowbowl football on an icy field and a frozen rugby tournament. Where else would you find an Outhouse Race, with enthroned beauties pulled down the street by their teammates, or a Bunny Boot Race with contestants wearing the large white boots that are the military's standard Arctic foot apparel? Keeping the general hilarity alive, even the five-mile foot race is run in costume. All this celebration can build up a big appetite and Rondy offers several special meals, including a Pioneer Pancake Breakfast, Salad Luncheon and Spaghetti Feed. Theatrical events include an old-fashioned melodrama, a presentation by the Alaska Repertory Theatre, a figure skating show and special film showings. Other musical and theatrical events are staged for children and teens.

Polar Bear Splash-In.

FEBRUARY/MARCH

Winter Carnival

Valdez, Alaska

Free
Contact: Valdez Chamber of Commerce, P.O. Box 512, Valdez, AK 99686

The hardiest participants of Winter Carnival plunge into the icy ocean waters off Alaska for a brisk swim. Other sturdy folk play softball on snowshoes or ride dogsleds. Not all people fight the onset of dreaded cabin fever with sports; some participate in talent shows, darts tournaments, a fashion show, fireworks, bonfires and a torch parade. Located in the furthest north ice-free port, Valdez is renowned for its alpine-like beauty. In midwinter its inhabitants shuck off their everyday lives and celebrate Alaska-style, and invite you to join them.

Snowshoe softball.

Crab Festival

Kodiak, Alaska

Free

Contact: Chamber of Commerce, P.O. Box 1485, Kodiak, AK 99615

Most residents of Kodiak are dependent upon the sea for their livelihood. Years ago, when the Crab Festival was initiated, they would harvest king crabs in winter and salmon in spring. The crabs have disappeared but the festival remains, along with the fishermen's hopes for the reappearance of this profitable crop. This celebration offers a carnival and some exciting sporting events, including a marathon, a mountain race, a water ball contest, an ultramarathon run over a 50-mile course and a survival suit race. It opens with a grand parade which is joined half an hour later by a costume parade for children. A pageant for the local Crab Festival Queen is held at the high school. A memorial service is conducted for fishermen lost during the last year, and the fleet parades past the ferry dock to receive its annual blessing.

JULY 4TH

4th of July

Seward, Alaska

Free

Contact: Chamber of Commerce, P.O. Box 756, Seward, AK 99664

Why would anyone run to the top of a 3,022-foot mountain and back down again? In Seward, such a run was started on a bet in 1915. The whole point was to make the trip—up the slopes, through rock-strewn gullies, across loose shale slides, frequently over snow and ice, and then down again—in less than an hour. Apparently it can be done, and athletes make this trip every year on the 4th of July. Recently a Women's Race has been added, and they, too, complete the course in under an hour. The Mount Marathon Race draws thousands of spectators and is the major attraction in Seward's festival. After the race, traffic is halted downtown and a parade marches through. Arts and crafts booths and other attractions dot the downtown area, and hungry revelers will find plenty of food booths.

JULY. 10 days

Golden Days

Fairbanks, Alaska

Free

Contact: Chamber of Commerce, P.O. Box 744446, Fairbanks, AK 99707

The Italian immigrant who first discovered gold in Fairbanks never dreamed he would become the inspiration of Alaska's largest summer festival. Each year his look-alike (chosen in a special contest) walks the streets with his mule for the annual re-creation of Pedro's Gold Weigh-In at the bank. Most of the events at this ten-day festival echo the flavor of the early 1900's when Alaska was a gold hunter's paradise. Gold panning and mining are demonstrated. 1902 fashions are paraded, a fake gambling hall is set up with phony money and real card games, an antique

Serving time in the 'slammer.'

air rally zooms through the skies, even beards and mustaches have their own contests. Many events are geared to children and include a Mutt Dog Show, a Kiddie Parade, a Magic Show and ice cream at 1900 prices. Throughout the entire festival, costumed deputies and floozies patrol the area to throw anyone not wearing a Golden Days button into a temporary slammer. Not surprisingly, no one seems to mind at all.

Eagle Council Grounds

Chilkat Bald Eagle Preserve, Haines, Alaska

Free
Contact: Chamber of Commerce, P.O. Box 518, Haines, AK
99827

The world's largest concentration of Bald Eagles can be viewed on the Chilkat River in Alaska. Portions of the river remain ice-free during the winter due to an unusual upwelling of warm water. These huge, emblematic birds congregate here to feed on spawned salmon. Viewers can sometimes see a hundred at a time. With the right equipment, and a little patience, they are easily photographed. The Alaska Chilkat Bald Eagle Preserve is an ideal place to see the birds. Highway pull-offs are located near the major gathering places. Although the wildlife site is undeveloped, facilities are available in the nearby town of Haines. Many of the birds breed here as well, and their tremendous nests (some weigh almost a ton) can be located in the preserve. More information, and showings of eagle films, can be found at the Haines Museum.

· CANADA ·

FEBRUARY, 5 days

Trapper's Festival

The Pas, Manitoba, Canada

Most events free
Contact: Travel Manitoba, Winnipeg, Manitoba, CAN R3C
0V8

Survival in the below-freezing weather of the northern Canadian woods wasn't easy for the fur trappers. Their lives and the success of their work depended upon certain skills emphasizing good sense and strength. In order to win the King Trapper title at Manitoba's Trapper Festival, the brawny entrants must compete in trap setting, ice fishing, tea boiling, pole climbing, tree felling, log sawing, canoe portaging

and other events modeled on the lives of last century's fur trappers. For instance, the winner must be able to carry 1,000 pounds of flour bags on his back, do moose calls and dance a jig in his moccasins. He must run eight miles in snowshoes under 55 minutes and drive a team of sled dogs over a 105-mile course in six hours. The central event of the festival is the three-day Championship Sled Dog Race with cash prizes for the winners. There are outdoor contests for women and the Fur Queen is crowned. Professional and local entertainers perform, and dances are held. A juried arts and crafts show attracts viewers, and beautiful fur fashions are modeled.

FEBRUARY. 8 days

Festival du Voyageur

Winnipeg, Manitoba, Canada

Admission charged to some events
Contact: Le Festival du Voyageur Inc., 768 Avenue Tache,
St. Boniface, Winnipeg, Manitoba, CAN R2C 2H4

Manitoba was once a large wilderness inhabited by Indians, fur trappers and a few settlers. It was governed at a distance by the Hudson Bay Company who hired *voyageurs* to travel the area on foot and by canoe, bringing in supplies and moving out the furs. The *voyageurs* and many of the settlers were French and there continues an influential population of Franco-Manitobans in the province today. Each winter they celebrate their heritage and the memory of the hard working, jovial *voyageurs*. Despite the distinctly cold weather, festival-goers line the streets to view the parade and its marching bands, decorated floats and costumed *voyageurs*.

A re-creation of a *voyageur* fort was built in Voyageur Park. Inside, costumed celebrants demonstrate fur-pressing, canoe making and other activities of the trappers. Inside the park are amusement rides, snow slides and dog sled rides for the children.

Musical and theatrical events take place at the park and in St. Boniface, Winnipeg's French suburb. Many sports events are scheduled, including a dog derby, a sled-dog pull, a hockey tournament, a rugby game on snow, a winter golf tournament on the frozen golf course, and basketball, swimming and wrestling contests. A storytelling event is planned. Educational exhibits and discussions of Franco-Manitoban folk heroes are also featured.

Salut à la prochaine!
See you next year!

FESTIVAL DU VOYAGEUR

JUNE AND JULY. 1 week, and 3 days

Potato Festivals

Grand Falls and Hartland, New Brunswick, Canada

Free

Contact: Special Events and Projects Coordinator, Tourism New Brunswick, P.O. Box 12345, Fredericton, New Brunswick, CAN E3B 5C3

The St. John River in western New Brunswick courses through a rich and beautiful agricultural valley. Two communities on the banks of the river celebrate with Potato Festivals. Both celebrations were born 25 years ago and they occur just a week apart. Many Grand Falls residents are Acadians, descended from the early French settlers. Their festival opens with special rodeo and skydiving demonstrations. The rodeo continues throughout the week accompanied by a Queen pageant, a Bavarian garden, wine cellar and a teen dance. A Canoe Derby is also held, and then a barbecue chicken supper. Saturday

brings a parade through downtown and a giant fireworks display at night. Hartland citizens are more likely to be from British backgrounds. Their festival features craft and commercial displays. A Queen is crowned in a pageant. The next day brings a children's doll carriage parade, local potato baking contest, a big homecoming supper and street dance. The last day features many old-fashioned country events from a chicken barbecue to a horse pull, and culminates in a grand fireworks display. Most visitors attend both festivals.

JULY 1ST. One week overlapping Canada Day

Folkfest

Victoria, B.C., Canada

Free

Contact: Inter-Cultural Association of Greater Victoria, P.O. Box 324, Victoria, B.C., CAN V8W 2N2

Canada is an interwoven tapestry of the world's ethnic cultures, and over 35 come together to celebrate Folkfest on the beautiful island of Victoria. Near the B.C. Provincial Museum an international village is set up in Centennial Square with kiosks representing different cultures and a stage where musicians and dancers perform throughout the week. Such varied foods as *adobo, parathas, spanokopitta, streudel, kaposta, sauerkraut* and *bunels* are sold. Each day is dedicated to a seperate group, with the second day devoted to children and seniors. Special movies are shown, clowns, puppets and school groups perform. The entire city of Victoria celebrates with special displays in shop windows and festive parties.

JULY. 10 days

Klondike Days

Edmonton, Alberta, Canada

Admission charged to some events
Contact: Convention and Tourism Authority, 9797 Jasper Ave.,
#104, Edmonton, Alberta, CAN T5J 1N9

In the 1890's Edmonton was the gateway to the Klondike, the last civilized town before the long trek to the goldfields. Would-be miners and soon-to-be casualties gathered their provisions here before the headlong rush towards gold in the Klondike River valley. Edmonton still remembers those years, and something of their hectic pace is echoed in the Klondike Days celebration. Nearly a million visitors attend the festival annually, and it was selected as one of the 'Top 100' events in America in 1983.

The event starts with a big parade the first evening. Floats, bands, and marching baton girls wind through downtown for a couple of hours. An Exposition runs daily with entertainment, horse racing, gold-panning, a carnival, the Golden Garter Casino, displays and exhibits. The Sourdough Raft Race on the North Saskatchewan River attracts an enthusiastic crowd.

Serious rafters race authentic craft for a prestigious cup and prize money. Later, a hilarious race of handmade craft tries to follow the same course. One afternoon the downtown streets are closed to allow the citizens to promenade in Gay '90s attire. Only the heartiest enter the King of the Klondike Contest featuring such he-man events as log rolling and arm wrestling. The Bathtub Races, Hairiest Chest in the West and Beard Growing Contests all appeal to those with a sense of humor. Other events include the mayor's honorary luncheon, a Sourdough Ball, a Klondike Kate songstress contest, and barbecues, breakfasts and picnics. A Junior Parade delights the children, along with a children's Dress-Up Contest and a Shoebox Float display. Marching bands from all over the West parade through downtown every weekday, then compete for major awards. Helpless maidens cringe in melodramas as the audience roots for the handsome heroes. Even the local buildings dress up in false storefronts to aid in re-creating the hectic era of the 1890's.

JULY. 5 days

SeaFest

Yarmouth, Nova Scotia, Canada

Most events free
Contact: Western Nova Scotia Festival Association, P.O. Box
577, Yarmouth, Nova Scotia, CAN B5A 4B4

The sea can't be ignored in Nova Scotia. Its breath affects the daily climate and it represents history, economy, food source, recreation and transportation to all who live here. Every summer natives of Yarmouth put on a SeaFest to celebrate their relationship with the sea. A grand Fish Feast is held and visitors can savour the harvest of the sea from dozens of booths set up in front of colorful Old World build-

ings. Rum running, dory and bike races are held. Crafts and antiques are sold. A street parade featuring the SeaFest Queen and her court winds through the town. In the evening, celebrants enjoy band concerts and dances.

Snowflake Handcraft Fair

North Battleford, Saskatchewan, Canada

Free
Contact: Eva Scott, Chairman, 1521 MacKenzie King Cross, North Battleford, Saskatchewan, CAN S9A 3C5

A local, hometown fair with artisans from the surrounding regions inhabits a shopping mall for this weekend. Visitors can view such crafts as wooden picture frames, polished rock jewelry, doll houses, hand-knit sweaters, crochet, sewing, ceramics, woodworks, clocks and handmade quilts. This juried show presents only handcrafted objects, nothing made from kits or catalogs. It has run since 1975, and successfully attracts buyers as well as those interested in learning the crafts.

ETHNIC CELEBRATIONS

The impulse to celebrate is universal. People can always think of a reason for a celebration, festival, jamboree or parade. Is the harvest ripening, have the snows been on the ground for months, does your art need displaying, is the old year ending or the new year beginning, do you want to keep the old times fresh in everyone's mind? Sometimes a celebration will seem to spring straight from the whimsical unconscious of a special population, other times its rituals have been carefully carried here from other lands. Some American celebrations date back to the 1700s, others are but a few years old. As long as the seasons change, and as long as people have the vitality to appreciate their world, they will continue to invent new festivals.

The most American of all celebrations are those paying tribute to specific ethnic heritages. America continues to be a melting pot of ethnic cultures. New populations migrate to this country in the centuries' old search for political stability and economic opportunity. At the same time, established groups celebrate their recollections of the Old Country and keep alive their traditions in exciting folkloric festivals. Everyday clothes are exchanged for lederhosen, kilts, a kimono, fur parka or serape. Second, third, fourth, even fifth generation Americans listen to the music of their forefathers and re-enact the celebrations of another land and another time.

At the heart of all ethnic celebrations are the people—those who have survived, who remember the old recipes, dances, stories, music and religions. Such festivals are a salute to the people and the persistence of their rich cultures. We can all understand these impulses and respond to the joyfulness of these occasions, no matter what ethnic groups live in our own family trees.

The following are special celebrations devoted to the many ethnic groups in this country. They are organized according to region, and are so diverse in their offerings they read like a listing from the Atlas. For further information, contact the addresses listed with each festival.

New England Ethnic Festivals

Connecticut
FESTA ITALIANA (Italian). Radio Station WRYM, Hartford, CT 06106. September.

BAGPIPE CONCERT AND SCOTTISH DANCING DAY. Dept. of Economic Development, 210 Washington St., Hartford, CT 06106. August.

Maine
SCOTTISH GAMES AND FESTIVAL. Chamber of Commerce, 59 Pleasant St., Brunswick, ME 04011. August.

FRANCO AMERICAN FESTIVAL (French). Chamber of Commerce, Lewiston, ME 04242. July.

Massachusetts
WORLD KIELBASA FESTIVAL (Polish). Chamber of Commerce, Chicopee, MA 01021. September.

FEAST OF THE BLESSED SACRAMENT (Portuguese). Chamber of Commerce, 628 Pleasant St., New Bedford, MA 02742. July/August.

New Hampshire
GATHERING OF THE SCOTTISH CLANS. Clans, Lincoln, NH 03251. September.

Rhode Island
OKTOBERFEST (German). Department of Economic Development, 7 Jackson Walkway, Providence, RI 02903. October.

COLUMBUS DAY FESTIVAL (Italian). Department of Economic Development, 7 Jackson Walkway, Providence, RI 02903. October.

Vermont
ETHNIC HERITAGE FESTIVAL (Various groups). Chamber of Commerce, Box 336, Barre, VT 05641. July.

OKTOBERFEST (German). Stowe Area Assoc., Main St., Box 1230, Stowe, VT 05672. September/October.

Mid-Atlantic Ethnic Festivals

Delaware
POLISH DAY. Delaware State Travel Service, P.O. Box 1401, Dover, DE 19901. June.

GREEK FESTIVAL. Holy Trinity Greek Orthodox Church, 808 N. Broom St., Wilmington, DE 19806. May/June.

ITALIAN FESTIVAL. St. Anthony's Church, 9th and Dupont Sts, Wilmington, DE 19805. June.

Maryland
ATHENIAN AGORA (Greek). Mary Kiladis, 24 W. Preston St, Baltimore, MD 21201. November.

CHINESE NEW YEAR FESTIVAL. Mrs. Herman Kim, Grace and St. Peter's Parish, 707 Park Ave, Baltimore, MD 21201. January.

OKTOBERFEST (German). Gaithersburg Community Center, 810 S. Frederick Ave., Gaithersburg MD 20760. October.

SPRINGS FOLK FESTIVAL (Pennsylvania Dutch). Festival, Springs, PA 15562. October.

SOUTHERN MARYLAND CELTIC FESTIVAL (Irish). Festival, Box 427, Bay View Dr., Chesapeake Beach, MD 20732. April.

ITALIAN SPRING FESTIVAL. Rev. Anthony Dal Balcon, 3800 Lottsford Vista Rd., Mitchellville, MD 20716. May.

SONGKRAN FESTIVAL (Thai). Wat Thai, 9033 Georgia Ave., Silver Spring, MD 20910. April.

New Jersey
HERITAGE FESTIVALS AT HOLMDEL (Various ethnic groups including Polish, Italian, Ukrainian, Jewish, Irish, etc.). Garden State Arts Center, Telegraph Hill Park, Holmdel, NJ 07733. Weekends in June and September.

New York
HELLENIC FESTIVAL (Greek). Chamber of Commerce, 107 Delaware Ave., Buffalo, NY 14202. May.

FRENCH FESTIVAL. Chamber of Commerce, Box 92, Cape Vincent, NY 13618. July.

CATSKILLS' IRISH FESTIVAL. Greene County Promotion Department, Box 467, Catskill, NY 12414. May.

ROBERT BURNS BANQUET (Scottish). Chamber of Commerce, Glens Falls, NY 12801. January.

GERMAN ALPS FESTIVAL. Exposition Planners, Bridge St., Hunter, NY 12442. July.

INTERNATIONAL CELTIC FESTIVAL (Irish). Exposition Planners, Bridge St., Hunter, NY 12442. August.

Pennsylvania

BAVARIAN SUMMER FESTIVAL. Festival, Box 90 Kempton, PA 19529. July.

GRAND IRISH JUBILEE. Jubilee, 123 S. Main St, Mahanoy City, PA 17948. September.

LITHUANIAN FESTIVAL. Joseph Yezulinas, 233 W. Oak St., Shenandoah, PA 17976. August.

POLISH FESTIVAL. Society of Shrine Volunteers, National Shrine of Our Lady of Czestochowa, Iron Hill and Ferry Rds, Doylestown, PA 18901. September.

FOLK FESTIVAL (Pennsylvanian Dutch). Festival, College Blvd. and Vine, Kutztown, PA 19530. June.

HIGHLAND GAMES (Scottish). Games, 1208 24th Ave., Altoona, PA 16601. September.

AMERICAN UKRAINIAN FESTIVAL. Holy Transfiguration Church, 240 Center St., Nanticoke, PA 18634. September.

PITTSBURGH FOLK FESTIVAL (Twenty-five different nationality groups). Festival, 610 Fifth Ave., Pittsburgh, PA 15219. May.

Washington, D.C.

ANNUAL SPRING FESTIVAL (Greek). Saints Constantine and Helen Greek Orthodox Church, 4115 16th St., NW, Washington, DC 20011. May

SPRING FESTIVAL (Chinese). Chinese Community Church, 1011 L St., NW, Washington, DC 20001. May.

SPRING FESTIVAL AND BAZAAR (Japanese). Japan-America Society of Washington, 1302 18th St., NW, Washington, DC 20036. June.

Southern Ethnic Festivals

Alabama

OKTOBERFEST (German). Washington Square, Mobile, AL 36601. October.

GREEK NIGHT BANQUET. Montgomery Civic Center, Montgomery, AL 36101. May.

AFRICAN EXTRAVAGANZA. Selma Convention Center, Selma, AL 36701. August.

Arkansas

BURNS' NICHT DINNER (Scottish). Alphin Dining Hall, Arkansas College, Batesville, AR 72501. January.

OKTOBERFEST (German). Chamber of Commerce, P.O. Box 1500, Hot Springs, AR 71901. October.

Florida

CANADIAN FESTIVAL. Chamber of Commerce, P.O. Box 2775, Daytona Beach, FL 32015. February/March.

DUNEDIN HEATHER AND THISTLE HOLIDAYS (Scottish). Chamber of Commerce, 434 Main St., Dunedin, FL 33528. March/April.

LEIF ERIKSEN DAY (Viking). Chamber of Commerce, 1910 NE Commercial St., Jensen Beach, FL 33457. October.

CZECHOSLOVAKIAN INDEPENDENCE DAY CELEBRATION. Vera Bucktan, Rt. 1, Box 242, Masaryktown, FL 33512. October.

OKTOBERFEST (German). Chamber of Commerce, P.O. Drawer 789, Melbourne, FL 32901. October.

LATIN AMERICAN FIESTA. Chamber of Commerce, P.O. Box 420, Tampa, FL 33601. March.

GREEK EPIPHANY DAY AND FESTIVAL. Chamber of Commerce, 112 S. Pinellas Ave, Tarpon Springs, FL 33589. January.

Georgia
ST. PATRICK'S FESTIVAL. Chamber of Commerce,
400 Bellevue Ave., Dublin, GA 31021. March.
OKTOBERFEST (German). Rousakis Plaza,
Savannah, GA 31402. October.

Kentucky
OKTOBERFEST (German). Don Brown, 502 W.
Sixth St, Covington, KT 41011. September.
OKTOBERFEST (German). Ed Bowles, 841 E.
Washington St., Louisville, KT 40206. October.

Louisiana
BASTILLE DAY (French). Anthony Fontenot, 905 W.
Sixth St., Kaplan, LA 70548. July.
FESTA D'ITALIA (Italian). Joseph Maselli, 1608
Salcedo St, New Orleans, LA 70125. October.
INTERNATIONAL ACADIAN FESTIVAL (Cajun).
Lester Hebert, Rt. 1, Box 146 A, Plaquemine, LA
70764. October.

Mississippi
PATTY'S PARTY OPEN HOUSE (Irish). Mississippi
Museum of Art, Jackson, MS 39205. March 17.

North Carolina
HIGHLAND GAMES AND GATHERING OF
SCOTTISH CLANS. Harris Prevost, Grandfather
Mountain, Linville, NC 28646. July.
SWISS BEAR FESTIVAL. Downtown Revitalization
Office, P.O. Box 597, New Bern, NC 28560.
October.
OKTOBERFEST (German). Jim Hammerle, 921
Tanglewood Dr., Cary, NC 27511. October.
FLORA MACDONALD HIGHLAND GAMES
(Scottish). Games, P.O. Box 547, Red Springs, NC
28377. October.
BLACK CULTURAL ARTS FESTIVAL. Recreation
Department, Southern Pines, NC 28387. July.

South Carolina
GREEK SPRING FESTIVAL. Alan Powell, Middleton
Place, Rt. 4, Charleston, SC 29407. May.

SCOTTISH GAMES AND HIGHLAND GATHERING.
Alan Powell, Middleton Place, Rt. 4, Charleston,
SC 29407. September.
A DAY IN FRANCE. Truluck Vineyards, Drawer
1265, Lake City, SC 29560. July.
CANADIAN-AMERICAN DAYS. Chamber of
Commerce, P.O. Box 2115, Myrtle Beach, SC
29577. March/April.
OKTOBERFEST (German). Chamber of Commerce,
Walhalla, SC 29691. October.

Virginia
SCOTTISH CHRISTMAS WALK. Elizabeth-Anne
Campagna, 418 S. Washington St., Alexandria,
VA 22314. December.
BLACK ARTS FESTIVAL. Visitor Center, 706
Caroline St., Fredericksburg, VA 22401. July.

West Virginia
BLACK CULTURAL FESTIVAL. Cultural Center,
Capitol Complex, Charleston, WV 25305. March.
ITALIAN HERITAGE FESTIVAL. Festival, 104 E.
Main St., Clarksburg, WV 26301. September.
SCOTTISH CLAN GATHERING AND HIGHLAND
GAMES. Games, 3310 Thomas Ave., Huntington,
WV 25705. June.

Mid-Western Ethnic Festivals

Illinois
JORDBRUKSDAGARNA (Swedish). Chamber of
Commerce, Bishop Hill, IL 61419. September
OLDE ENGLISH FAIRE. Jubilee College State Park,
Brimfield, IL 61517. June.
CHINATOWN AUGUST MOON FESTIVAL.
Visitors Bureau, Chicago Assoc. of Commerce
and Industry, 130 South Michigan Ave.,
Chicago, IL 60603. August.
DUTCH DAYS FESTIVAL. Chamber of Commerce,
Box 253, Fulton, IL 61252. May.
SWEDISH DAYS. Chamber of Commerce, P.O. Box
481, Geneva, IL 60134. June.
LATINO FESTIVAL. Chamber of Commerce,
Waukegan, IL 60085. July.
SCOTTISH FAIR. Winnetka Community House,
620 Lincoln Ave., Winnetka, IL 60093. October.

Indiana

SWISS DAYS. Randy Beer, 125 N. Jefferson St., Berne, IN 46711. July.

LITTLE ITALY FESTIVAL. Rita Muciarelli, 849 North St., Clinton, IN 47842. September.

HERBFEST (German). Judy Olinger, Box 28, Huntingburg, IN 47542. October.

OKTOBERFEST (German). German-American Klub, 8602 South Meridian St., Indianapolis, IN 46217. September.

ST. BENNO FEST (Old Bavarian). Bob Swan 401 E. Michigan St., Indianapolis, IN 46204. March.

GRECIAN FESTIVAL. Michael G. Kapnas, Twin Towers (South), Suite 516, Merrillville, IN 46410. July.

LA FESTA (Italian). A.A. Greco, 6695 Broadway, Merrillville, IN 46410. June.

SWISS ALPINE FESTIVAL. Bob Bloem, R.R. 1, Box 9A, Vevay, IN 47043. August.

Iowa

CZECH VILLAGE FESTIVAL. Festival, 59 16th Ave. SW, Cedar Rapids, IA 52404. September.

SCANDINAVIAN DAGER CELEBRATION. Festival, 120 N. Lucas St., Eagle Grove, IA 50533. June.

SAINT PATRICK'S DAY CELEBRATION (Irish). Festival, Emmetsburg, IA 50536. March.

CZECH FOLK FEST. Folk Fest, Traer, IA 50675. July.

Kansas

MEXICAN INDEPENDENCE CELEBRATION. Chamber of Commerce, Kansas City, KS 66110. September.

SVENSK HYLLINGFEST (Swedish). Chamber of Commerce, Lindsborg, KS 67456. October in odd numbered years.

OKTOBERFEST (German). Chamber of Commerce, Manhattan, KS 66502. October.

MEXICAN FIESTA. Our Lady of Guadalupe Church, Topeka, KS 66601. July.

SAINT PATRICK'S DAY CELEBRATION AND PARADE (Irish). Chamber of Commerce, Wichita, KS 67277. March 17.

ASIAN DAY FESTIVAL. Chamber of Commerce, Wichita, KS 67277. September.

AFTER-HARVEST CZECH FESTIVAL. Chamber of Commerce, Wilson, KS 67490. July.

Michigan

HIGHLAND FESTIVAL (Scottish). Festival, P.O. Box 506, Alma, MI 48801. May.

IRISH WEEKEND. Chamber of Commerce, Bellaire, MI 49615. March.

POLISH FESTIVAL DAYS. Festival, 206 N. Walker St., Bronson, MI 49028. July.

BAVARIAN FESTIVAL (German). Chamber of Commerce, 635 S. Main St., Frankenmuth, MI 48734. June.

DANISH FESTIVAL. Festival, 327 S. Lafayette St., Greenville, MI 48838. August.

Minnesota

OKTOBERFEST (German). Aitkin Independent Age, 213 Minnesota Ave. North, Aitkin, MN 56413. October.

DANISH DAYS. Danish American Fellowship, 4200 Cedar Ave., Minneapolis, MN 55407. June.

DUTCH FESTIVAL. Chamber of Commerce, 230 Trosky St., Edgerton, MN 56128. July.

FINNAFFAIR (Finnish). Scandinavia Today, 1200 First Bank Place East, Box 522, Minneapolis, MN 55480. September.

SVENSKARNAS DAG (Swedish). Festival, 1605 Louisiana Ave., Minneapolis, MN 55426. June.

SYTTENDE MAI (Norwegian). Jim Johnson, Scandian Imports, LaSalle Court, 33 S. Eighth St., Minneapolis, MN 55402. May.

UKRAINIAN DAY. Luba Menshena, 1054 Southeast 14th Ave., Minneapolis, MN 55414. August.

KOLACKY DAYS (Czechoslovakian). Montgomery Area Community Club, 303 Northwest Fourth St., Montgomery, MN 56069. July/August.

KASITYONAYTTELY FESTIVAL (Finnish). Finn Creek Ulkmuseo, New York Mills, MN 56567. September.

IRISH FESTIVAL. Minnesota Gaelic Cultural Committee, 1450 Bidwell St., West St. Paul, MN 55118. October.

AEBLESKIVER DAY (Danish). Commercial Club, 101 McGoudy St., Tyler, MN 56178. June.

BERNE SWISSFEST. Festival, Box 36, West Concord, MN 55985. August.

POLISH HERITAGE DAYS. Polish Heritage Society, 625 E. Fourth St., Winona, MN 55987. May.

Missouri

MAIFEST (German). Tourist Headquarters, Box 88, Hermann, MO 65041. May.

SAINT PAT'S CELEBRATION (Irish). Public Information Office, Univ. of Missouri, Rolla, MO 65401. March.

BADENFEST (German). Convention and Visitors Bureau, 1300 Convention Plaza, St. Louis, MO 63103. September.

JOUR DE FETE (French). Chamber of Commerce, Box 166, Ste. Genevieve, MO 63670. August.

Nebraska

CZECH FESTIVAL. Ron Vavrina, Box M, Clarkson, NE 68629. June.

SWEDISH DAYS CELEBRATION. Festival, Box 183, Holdredge, NE 68949. June.

GRECIAN FESTIVAL. St. John's Greek Orthodox Church, 602 Park Avenue, Omaha, NE 68105. August.

SANTA LUCIA FESTIVAL (Italian). Omaha Visitors Bureau, Omaha-Douglas Civic Center, Suite 1200, 1819 Farnam St., Omaha, NE 68183. July/August.

ST. PATRICK'S DAY CELEBRATION (Irish). Chamber of Commerce, 430 East Douglas St., O'Neill, NE 68763. March 17.

SWEDISH FESTIVAL. Stromsburg Commercial Club, Box 453, Stromsburg, NE 68666. June.

North Dakota

OKTOBERFEST (German). Chamber of Commerce, 425 S. Seventh St., Bismarck, ND 58501. September.

NORSK HOSTEFEST (Norwegian). Chamber of Commerce, P.O. Drawer 940, Minot, ND 58701. October.

Ohio

OLD WORLD OKTOBERFEST (German). Geauga Lake Park, 1060 Aurora Rd, OH 44202. September.

GRECIAN FESTIVAL. Ann Economos, 421 18th St. NW, Canton, OH 44703. August.

SLAVIC VILLAGE HARVEST FESTIVAL. James Matuszak, 3739 East 57th St., Cleveland, OH 44105. September.

STS. CONSTANTINE AND HELEN GRECIAN
FESTIVAL. George Fikaris, 3352 Mayfield Rd.,
Cleveland Heights, OH 44118. September.
ISRAEL FESTIVAL. Jewish Center, 1125 College
Ave., Columbus, OH 43209. May.
ST. JOHN'S ITALIAN FESTIVAL. Benny Andreoni,
5306 Poplarwood St., Columbus, OH 43229.
October.
WELSH HERITAGE DAYS. Bob Evans Farm, P.O.
Box 330, Rio Grande, OH 45674. June.
OHIO SWISS FESTIVAL. Don Sprankle, P.O. Box
249, Sugarcreek, OH 44681. October.

South Dakota

SCHMECKFEST (Mennonites, Hutterites and Low
Germans). Festival, Freeman, SD 57029. March.
GERMAN SUMMERFEST. Convention-Visitors
Bureau, Box 747, 444 Mount Rushmore Rd. N.,
Rapid City, SD 57709. August.
CZECH DAYS. Chamber of Commerce, Tabor, SD
57063. June.

Wisconsin

HOLLAND FESTIVAL (Dutch). Festival, Box GD,
Cedar Grove, WI 53013. July.
FIESTA MEXICANA. Summerfest Office, 200 N.
Harbor Dr., Milwaukee, WI 53202. August.
GERMAN FEST. Summerfest Office, 200 N. Harbor
Dr., Milwaukee, WI 53202. August.
GREEK FESTIVAL. Greater Milwaukee Convention
and Visitors Bureau, 756 N. Milwaukee St.,
Milwaukee, WI 53202. July.
JUNETEENTH DAY (Black Culture). Greater
Milwaukee Convention and Visitors Bureau, 756
N. Milwaukee St., Milwaukee, WI 53202. June.
LA KERMESSE DE LA BASTILLE (French). Greater
Milwaukee Convention and Visitors Bureau. 756
N. Milwaukee St., Milwaukee, WI 53202. July.
HEIDI FESTIVAL (Swiss). Chamber of Commerce,
Box 713, New Glarus, WI 53574. June.
SYTTENDE MAI (Norwegian). Chamber of
Commerce, 143 West Main St., Stoughton, WI
53589. May.

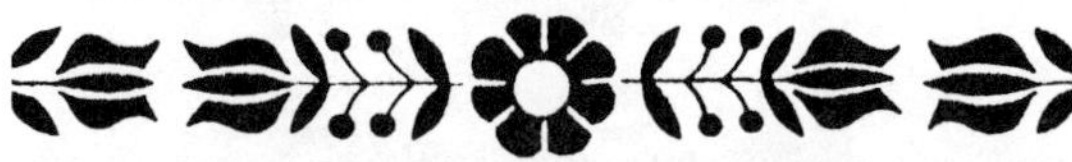

Southwestern Ethnic Festivals

Arizona

MEXICAN INDEPENDENCE DAY. Chamber of
Commerce, Nogales, AZ 85621. September 16.

New Mexico

GRECIAN FESTIVAL. St. George Greek Orthodox
Church, Albuquerque, NM 87103. October.
OKTOBERFEST (German). Festival, Angel Fire
Resort, NM 87718. October.
BLACK ASSOCIATED STUDENTS ETHNIC
CELEBRATION. New Mexico State University,
Las Cruces, NM 88001. February.

Oklahoma

ITALIAN FESTIVAL. Chamber of Commerce, Box
759, McAlester, OK 74501. May.
KOLACHE FESTIVAL (Czechoslovakian). Jack Smith,
Prague, OK 74865. May.

Texas

CHARRO DAYS FIESTA (Mexican). Festival, Box
1904, Brownsville, TX 78520. February.
A NIGHT IN OLD FREDERICKSBURG (German).
Chamber of Commerce, Box 506, Fredericksburg,
TX 78624. July.
JUNETEENTH BLUES FESTIVAL (Black Culture).
SUM Concerts, 3323 Yoakum St., Houston, TX
77006. June.
WURSTFEST (German). Festival, Box 180, New
Braunfels, TX 78130. October/November.

MEXICAN HERITAGE FIESTA. Chamber of
Commerce, 4749 Twin City Highway, Port
Arthur, TX 77640. September.
ST. PATRICK'S DAY CELEBRATION (Irish). Jackie
Orr, 306 North Presa, Suite 2, San Antonio, TX
78205. March.
WESTFEST (Czechoslavakian). Westfest, Box 65,
West, TX 76691. September.

Rocky Mountain Ethnic Festivals

Colorado
FASCHING (German). Chamber of Commerce, P.O.
Box 655, Georgetown, CO 80444. February.

Idaho
BASQUE PICNIC, STREET DANCE, AND HOLIDAY
DANCE. TOURIDAHO, State Capital Build.,
Room 108, Boise, ID 83720. July.

Montana
HERBSTFEST (German). Chamber of Commerce,
Box 395, Laurel, MT 59044. September.

Nevada
WHITE PINE BASQUE FESTIVAL. Betty Fielding, 8
Elysium Dr., Ely, NV 89301. July
GREEK FESTIVAL. Sands Hotel, Las Vegas, NV
89109. October.
ITALIAN FESTIVAL. Eldorado Hotel, Reno, NV
89101. October.
BASQUE FESTIVAL. Chamber of Commerce, 48
West Winnemucca Blvd., Winnemucca, NV
89445. June.

Utah
MIDWAY SWISS DAYS. Utah Travel Council,
Council Hall/Capital Hill, Salt Lake City, UT
84114. September.
OKTOBERFEST (German). Utah Travel Council,
Council Hall/Capital Hill, Salt Lake City, UT
84114. September.
GREEK FESTIVAL. Holy Trinity Greek Orthodox
Church, 279 South Third West, Salt Lake City,
UT 84101. September.

VIVA LA FIESTA (Latin American). Utah Travel
Council, Council Hall/Capitol Hill, Salt Lake City,
UT 84114. September.

Wyoming
OKTOBERFEST (Bavarian). Dean Duncan, 1300
Howell Ave., Worland, WY 82401. September.

Pacific Ethnic Festivals

California
SWEDISH FESTIVAL. Chamber of Commerce, Box
515, Kingsburg, CA 93631. May.
OKTOBERFEST (German). Chamber of Commerce,
Box 386, Lodi, CA 95241. October.
CINCO DE MAYO (Mexican). Visitors and
Convention Bureau, 505 South Flower St., Los
Angeles, CA 90071. May.
CHERRY BLOSSOM FESTIVAL (Japanese).
Convention and Visitors Bureau, 1390 Market
St., San Francisco, CA 94102. April.

CHINESE NEW YEAR CELEBRATION. Convention and Visitors Bureau, 1390 Market St., San Francisco, CA 94102. February.

ST. PATRICK'S FROLIC (Irish). Convention and Visitors Bureau, 1390 Market St., San Francisco, CA 94102. March 17.

LA FIESTA (Spanish and Mexican). Chamber of Commerce, 1039 Chorro St., San Luis Obispo, CA 93401. Third weekend in May.

SCOTTISH GATHERING AND GAMES. Chamber of Commerce, 637 First St., Santa Rosa, CA 95404. September.

CHINESE NEW YEAR CELEBRATION. Convention and Visitors Bureau, 46 West Fremont St., Stockton, CA 95202. February.

Oregon

SCANDINAVIAN FESTIVAL. Festival, P.O. Box 5, Junction City, OR 97448. August.

OKTOBERFEST (German). Oktoberfest Assoc., Box 431, Mount Angel, OR 97362. September.

ALPENFEST (Swiss). Tourist Committee, Box 358, Joseph, OR 97846. September.

Washington

KELSO HILANDER SUMMER FESTIVAL (Scottish). Chamber of Commerce, Box 58, Kelso, WA 98626. June.

MAI FEST (German). Festival, Box 313, Leavenworth, WA 98826. May.

ODESSA DEUTSCHES FEST (German). Chamber of Commerce, Odessa, WA 99159. September.

GREEK FESTIVAL. Chamber of Commerce, Box 433, Soap Lake, WA 98851. May.

Alaskan, Hawaiian & Canadian Ethnic Festivals

Alaska

LITTLE NORWAY FESTIVAL. Festival, Box 1309, Petersburg, AK 99833. May.

Hawaii

INTERNATIONAL FESTIVAL OF THE PACIFIC (Multi-ethnic). Visitors Bureau, 2270 Kalakaua Av., Suite 801, Honolulu, HI 96815. July.

CHERRY BLOSSOM FESTIVAL (Japanese). Japanese Junior Chamber of Commerce, 2645 South Beretania St., Honolulu, HI 96813. February thru April.

FIESTA FILIPINA (Phillipine). United Filipino Council of Hawaii, P.O. Box 457, Pearl City, HI 96782. July.

NARCISSUS FESTIVAL (Chinese). Chinese Chamber of Commerce, 42 North King St., Honolulu, HI 96817. January thru February, around Chinese New Year.

Canada

GREEK FOOD FESTIVAL. Tourism British Columbia, Robson Square, 800 Robson St., Vancouver, B.C., CAN V6Z 2C6. May.

UKRAINIAN FESTIVAL. Tourism British Columbia, Robson Square, 800 Robson St., Vancouver, B.C., CAN V6Z 2C6. April/May.

ISLENDINGADAGURINN (Icelandic Festival).
Festival, Box 1499, Gimli, Man., CAN R0C 1B0.
August.

OKTOBERFEST (German). Travel Manitoba, Dept.
2001, Winnipeg, Man., CAN R3C 0V8.
September.

MABOU CEILIDH (Scottish). Dept. of Tourism, P.O.
Box 130, Halifax, N.S., CAN B3J 2M7. June/July.

NOVA SCOTIA GAELIC MOD (Scottish). Dept. of
Tourism, P.O. Box 130, Halifax, N.S., CAN B3J
2M7. August.

CLARE ACADIAN FESTIVAL. Dept. of Tourism,
P.O. Box 130, Halifax, N.S., CAN B3J 2M7. July.

L'ARDOISE ACADIAN FESTIVAL. Dept. of
Tourism, P.O. Box 130, Halifax, N.S., CAN B3J
2M7. July.

OKTOBERFEST (German). Ministry of Tourism,
Queen's Park, Toronto, Ont., CAN M7A 2E1.
October.

ST. ROCCO ITALIAN FESTIVAL. St. Peter's Church,
756 Maxwell St., Sarnia, Ont., CAN N7T 5E8.
August.

ST. JEAN BAPTISTE ACTIVITY DAYS (French).
Centre Cultural LaRonde, 32 Mountjoy St. N,
Timmins, Ont., CAN P4N 4V6. June.

BON ODORI FESTIVAL (Japanese). Toronto
Buddhist Church, 918 Bathurst St., Toronto,
Ont., CAN M4K 1V9. July.

BRITISH NIGHT. Visitor Services, P.O. Box 940,
Charlottetown, Prince Edward Island, CAN C1A
7M5. June.

NATIVE AMERICAN CELEBRATIONS

Native Americans celebrate their traditions and memories in festivals all around the country. The following list is a sample of these events. They include a fascinating medley of pow wows, feasts, festivals, exhibitions, dances, round-ups and fairs. If you need more information, contact the address listed with each festival.

New England Indian Festivals

Rhode Island
NARRAGANSETT INDIAN FALL FESTIVAL. Rhode Island Department of Economic Development, 7 Jackson Walkway, Providence, RI 02903. October.

Mid-Atlantic Indian Festivals

Delaware
NANTICOKE INDIAN POW WOW. Delaware State Travel Service, 630 State College Rd., P.O. Box 1401, Dover, DE 19901. September.

New York

IROQUOIS INDIAN FESTIVAL. Chamber of
Commerce, Box 352, Cobleskill, NY 12043.
September.

SENECA NATION INDIAN FALL FESTIVAL.
Chamber of Commerce, Box 45, Gowanda, NY
14070. September.

MOUNTAIN EAGLE INDIAN FESTIVAL. Exposition
Planners, Bridge St, Hunter, NY 12442.
September.

SHINNECOCK INDIAN POW WOW. Chamber of
Commerce, 76 Main St., Southampton, NY
11968. September.

Southern Indian Festival

Alabama

CREEK INDIAN THANKSGIVING DAY
HOMECOMING AND POW WOW. Creek Indian
Nation, Rt. 3, Box 243-A, Atmore, AL 36502.
November.

Georgia

INDIAN DANCE FESTIVAL AND PIONEER FAIR.
Festival, 93 Ivy Trail, Northeast, Atlanta, GA
30342. March.

Florida

SEMINOLE INDIAN TRIBAL FAIR. Seminole Tribe
of Florida, 6073 Sterling Rd., Hollywood, FL
33024. February.

Louisiana

UNITED AMERICAN INDIAN POW WOW.
Secretary, Indian Angels, P.O. Box 528883, Baton
Rouge, LA 70805. June.

Mississippi

CHOCTAW INDIAN FAIR. Chamber of Commerce,
P.O. Box 51, Philadelphia, MS 39350. July.

North Carolina

NATIVE AMERICAN FESTIVAL & FALL POW
WOW. Schiele Museum of Natural History, 1500
E. Garrison Blvd., Gastonia, NC 28052. October.

CHEROKEE FALL FESTIVAL. Festival, Rt. 1,
Whittier, NC 28789. October.

Midwestern Indian Festivals

Indiana

TRAIL OF COURAGE RENDEZVOUS. Fulton
County Historical Society, 7th and Pontiac Sts.,
Rochester, IN 46975. September.

Iowa

MESQUAKIE INDIAN POW WOW. Pow Wow,
Indian Settlement, Tama, IA 52339. August.

Kansas

MID AMERICA INDIAN POW WOW. Chamber of
Commerce, Wichita, KS 67201. July.

Minnesota

MAHKATO MDEWAKANTON POW WOW.
Festival, MSU, Box 61, Mankato, MN 56001.
September.

North Dakota

UNITED TRIBES POW WOW. United Tribes
Educational Technical Center, 3315 S. Airport
Rd., Bismarck, ND 58501. September.

South Dakota

FORT THOMPSON FAIR AND POW WOW. Crow Creek Indian Reservation, Fort Thompson, SD 57339. August.

ROSEBUD SIOUX FAIR AND POW WOW. Rosebud Reservation, Rosebud, SD 57570. August.

Wisconsin

INDIAN POW WOW. Chamber of Commerce, Box 112, Black River Falls, WI 54615. May.

Southwestern Indian Festivals

Arizona

O'ODHAM TASH, CASA GRANDE INDIAN DAYS. Chamber of Commerce, 201 E. Fourth St., Casa Grande, AZ 85222. February.

PAPAGO ALL INDIAN FAIR. Papago, P.O. Box 837, Sells, Az 85634. November.

New Mexico

CANDELERIA DAY, NEW YEAR'S DAY CELEBRATION, and THREE KINGS DAY CELEBRATION. P.O. Box 70, Cochiti Pueblo, NM 87041. February, January and January.

GO-CHEE-YA and LITTLE BEAVER ROUNDUP. P.O. Box 313, Dulce, NM 87528. September and July.

SAN DIEGO FEAST. At Jemez and Tesuque Pueblos. P.O. Box 78 Jemez Pueblo, NM 87024. Both November.

OUR LADY OF GUADALUPE FEAST DAY. Jemez Pueblo: P.O. Box 78, Jemez Pueblo, NM 87024. Nambe Pueblo: Rt. 1, Box 117-BB Santa Fe, NM 87501. Pojoaque Pueblo: Rt 1, Box 71, Santa Fe, NM 87501. December.

Papago fry bread is popular at Southwestern celebrations.

SAN JOSE FEAST DAYS. P.O. Box 194, Laguna, NM 87026. March and September.

CANDELARIA DAY. Picuris Pueblo: P.O. Box 228, Penasco, NM 87553. San Felipe Pueblo: Box 308 San Felipe Pueblo, NM 87001. Santo Domingo Pueblo: Gen. Deliv., Santo Domingo Pueblo, NM 87052. February.

SAN FELIPE FEAST DAY. San Felipe Pueblo: Box 308, Algodones, NM 87001. May.

SAN ILDEFONSO FEAST DAY. San Ildefonso Pueblo: Box 315-A, Santa Fe, NM 87501. January.

SAN JUAN FEAST DAY. Box 1099, San Juan Pueblo, NM 87566. June.

SANTA ANA FEAST DAY. Box 37, Santa Ana Pueblo, Bernalillo, NM 87004. July.

PUYE CLIFFS CEREMONIAL. Box 580, Santa Clara Pueblo, Espanola, NM 87532. July.

SANTO DOMINGO FEAST DAY. Gen. Deliv., Santo Domingo Pueblo, NM 87052. August.

SAN GERONIMO FEAST DAY. Box 1846, Taos Pueblo, NM 87571. September.

ZUNI TRIBAL FAIR. Box 339, Zuni Pueblo, NM 87382. August.

Oklahoma

AMERICAN INDIAN EXPOSITION. Chamber of Commerce, Box 266, Anadarko, OK 73005. August.

KIAMICHI OWA CHITO FESTIVAL OF THE FOREST. Chamber of Commerce 13 N. Central St., Idabel, OK 74745. June.

SEQUOYAH INTERNATIONAL POW WOW.
Chamber of Commerce, P.O. Box 972, Elk City,
OK 73644. June.
CHEROKEE NATIONAL HOLIDAY. P.O. Box 948,
Tahlequah, OK 74464. September.
TULSA POW WOW. Kenneth Anquoe, 1409 S.
Darlington St., Tulsa, OK 74112. July.

Texas

SAINT ANTHONY'S DAY CELEBRATION and
THANKSGIVING WEEKEND. Tigua Indian
Reservation, Box 17579, El Paso, TX 79917. June
and November.
INDIAN POW WOW AND INTERNATIONAL
TEPEE COMPETITION. Traders Village, 2602
Mayfield Rd., Grand Prairie, TX 75051.
September.

Rocky Mountain Indian Festivals

Colorado

KOSHARE INDIAN DANCES. Chamber of
Commerce, Box 408, La Junta, CO 81050.
August.

Idaho

TALMAKS CAMP MEETING. Chamber of
Commerce, Craigmont, ID 83523. July.
SHOSHONE-BANNOCK INDIAN DAY. Fort Hall, ID
83203. October.
PI-NEE-WAU DAYS. Lapwai, ID 83540. August.
SUN DANCE. Pocatello, ID 83201. July.
WHAA-LAA DAYS. Worley, ID 83876. TourIdaho,
State Capitol Building, Room 108, Boise, ID
83720. July.

Nevada

ALL-INDIAN RODEO AND PIONEER DAYS.
Chamber of Commerce, 30 W. Williams Ave.,
Fallon, NV 89406. July.

Utah

UTE TRIBAL BEAR DANCE. Utah Travel Council,
Council Hall/Capitol Hill, Salt Lake City, UT
84114. April.

Wyoming

INDIAN TRIBAL POW WOWS AND SUN DANCES.
BIA, Programs Office, Fort Washakie, WY 82514.
July.

Alaskan & Canadian Indian Festivals

Alaska

WORLD ESKIMO AND INDIAN OLYMPIC GAMES.
Convention and Visitors Bureau. 550 First Ave.,
Fairbanks, AK 99701. July.
CHILKAT INDIAN DANCERS. Alaska Indian Arts,
Box 271, Haines, AK 99827. June through
September.
NORTHWEST NATIVE TRADE FAIR. Arctic Circle
Chamber of Commerce, Box 284, Kotzebue, AK
99752. July.

Canada

LAC LA BICHE POW WOW DAYS. Travel Alberta,
Box 2500, Edmonton, Alberta, CAN T5J 2Z4.
July/August.
NATIVE INDIAN ARTS AND CRAFTS SHOW.
Southwestern British Columbia Tourist Assoc,
P.O. Box 94449, Richmond, British Columbia,
CAN V6Y 2A8. August.
OPASQUIA INDIAN DAYS. Travel Manitoba,
Department 2001, Winnipeg, Manitoba, CAN
R3C 0V8. August.
SIX NATIONS INDIAN PAGEANT. William Smith,
RR No. 6, Hagersville, Ontario, CAN N0A 1H0.
August.
WIKWEMIKONG INDIAN POW WOW. Unceded
Indian Reserve, Box 112, Wikwemikong, Ontario,
CAN P0P 2J0. July/August.
SAKIMAY INDIAN POW WOW. Sakimay Band
Office, Box 339, Grenfell, Saskatchewan, CAN
S0G 2B0. June.

Photo Credits

NEW ENGLAND
Snodeo: BLYTHE PHOTO, *Rangeley, ME*
Fisherman's Festival: EMILY LEE REILLY; ROBERT NICOLL PHOTO
Wool Days: ROBERT S. ARNOLD
Lake Champlain Discovery Festival: VERMONT TRAVEL DIV.
Music Mountain Chamber Music Festival: GARY GUNDERSON
Pilgrim Wedding: PLIMOTH PLANTATION PHOTO
The Maine Festival: GEORGE RILEY PHOTO

MID-ATLANTIC
Winter Carnival: DAVID VERNER
Cherry Blossom Festival: WASHINGTON CONVENTION & VISITOR'S ASSOC.
Chautauqua Institution: GEORGE S. MORGAN
New York Street Fairs: NEW YORK CONVENTION & VISITOR'S BUREAU
Wildfowl Carving & Art Exhibition: WARD FOUNDATION, *Salisbury, MD*
Village Hawllowe'en Parade: AMY GELFAND

SOUTH
Old Salem Christmas: OLD SALEM RESTORATION, *Winston-Salem, N.C.*
Christmas Island: JEKYLL ISLAND AUTHORITY, *Jekyll Island, GA*
Reelfoot Eagle Tours: TENNESSEE TOURIST DEVELOPMENT
Mardi Gras: DONN YOUNG
Peanut Frolic: GEORGIA AGRIRAMA
Shenandoah Apple Blossom Festival: HALLMARK PHOTOGRAPHY
New Orleans Jazz & Heritage Festival: MICHAEL P. SMITH
Billy Bowlegs Festival: FLORIDA PHOTO
Chincoteague Annual Carnival & Pony Penning: RAY WALKER, JR.
Festivals Acadiens: JAY ELLEDGE
Corn Island Storytelling Festival: THERESA L. MONTGOMERY
National Storytelling Festival: TENNESSEE TOURIST DEVELOPMENT
Perryville Battlefield Celebration & Re-Enactment: KENTUCKY DEPARTMENT OF TOURISM

MIDWEST

St. Louis Storytelling Festival: UNIVERSITY OF MISSOURI, *St. Louis, MO*
A Taste of Bloomington: DAVE REPP
Tom Sawyer Days: BOB GREENLEE
Festa Italiana: DR. EDWARD F. LEONE
Douglas County Historical Steam Festival: FRED NOLAN
Minnesota Renaissance Festival: JOHN HAGERMAN
King Turkey Day: LEW HUDSON
Cheese Days: LARRY LINDGREN
Feast of the Hunter's Moon: SHIRLEY SEREQUE

SOUTHWEST

Hopi & Navaho Craftsman Exhibitions: MNA PHOTO
Albuquerque Int'l. Balloon Fiesta: PATRICIA BEHRMANN
Bat Flight Breakfast: NATIONAL PARK SERVICE
Will Rogers Day: OKLAHOMA TOURISM, FRED W. MARVEL
Inter-Tribal Indian Ceremonial: BOB PALUZZI

ROCKY MOUNTAIN

Art on the Green: DON SAUSSER
Park City Art Festival: CAPTIVE IMAGE, DAVID QUIST

PACIFIC

Doo-Dah Parade: JOE MESSINGER, WALT MANCINI
Oregon Shakespearean Festival: HANK KRANZLER
Cinco de Mayo: RICHARD DIAZ
Mule Days: WALTER L. RICKELL ©1973 *Horse & Rider Magazine*
Myth California Pageant: BOB MARSHAK
Summer Solstice Parade: CARA MOORE
Gilroy Garlic Festival: CHRIS MURPHY
Old Spanish Days: CARA MOORE
Danish Days: KING MERRILL
Wooden Boat Festival: DYANNA WOLCOTT
Street Scene Festival: DAVID BECKER
Monterrey Jazz Festival: TOM COPI

HAWAII, ALASKA & CANADA

Valdez Winter Carnival: VALDEZ VANGUARD
Eagle Council Grounds: W. PERRY CONWAY, COURTESY NATIONAL AUDUBON SOCIETY
Northern Manitoba Trappers' Festival: TRAVEL MANITOBA

ETHNIC & NATIVE AMERICAN

Danish Days: KING MERRILL; CRAIG BENSON

About the Author

JUDY YOUNG, besides being an avid frequenter of parades, festivals and celebrations and a craft teacher, is also co-author of BIRDWATCHING: *A Guide for Beginners.* She lives in Santa Barbara, where many American holidays begin and end.